W9-BYK-088

Also by Kevin Brockmeier

A Few Seconds of Radiant Filmstrip

A Few Seconds of Radiant Filmstrip

A Memoir of Seventh Grade

Kevin Brockmeier

Pantheon Books, New York

Copyright © 2014 by Kevin Brockmeier

All rights reserved. Published in the United States by Pantheon Books, a division of Random House LLC, New York, and in Canada by Random House of Canada Limited, Toronto, Penguin Random House companies.

Pantheon Books and colophon are registered trademarks of Random House LLC.

Portions of this book have previously appeared, in slightly different form, in *The Oxford American* (Summer 2011) as "Seventh Grade," in *Gulf Coast* (Summer/Fall 2013) as "Two Days in Seventh Grade," in *The Oxford American* (Summer 2012) as "More Seventh Grade," in *Granta Online* (January 2014) as "The Case of the Missing Miss Vincent," in *The Georgia Review* (Winter 2013) as "Dead Last Is a Kind of Second Place," and in *Interfictions* (Fall 2013) as "The Plans, The Blueprints."

Library of Congress Cataloging-in-Publication Data
Brockmeier, Kevin.
A Few Seconds of Radiant Filmstrip : a Memoir of Seventh Grade /
Kevin Brockmeier.
pages   cm
ISBN 978-0-307-90898-8 (hardback) ISBN 978-0-307-90899-5 (eBook)
1. Brockmeier, Kevin—Childhood and youth.   2. Authors, American—
Biography.   3. Boys—United States—Biography.   4. Preteens—
United States—Social life and customs.   I. Title.
PS3602.R63Z46 2014   813'.6—dc23   [B]   2013031895

www.pantheonbooks.com

Cover design and illustration by Paul Sahre

Printed in the United States of America
First Edition
2   4   6   8   9   7   5   3   1

Sometimes one who thinks himself incomplete is merely young.

—Italo Calvino

*A Few Seconds of
Radiant Filmstrip*

. . . .

He feels like a different person. There he is, scaling the bluff behind Mazzio's Pizza, bracing his sneakers against chunks of stone and the whip handles of baby trees, twenty-five feet above the parking lot. He could be a stuntman, a daredevil, almost anything. He clasps a rock, the kind made from hundreds of chalky plates, and reaches for another. His hand finds a tuft of grass instead. Then he snatches at a pine sapling and it separates from the ground in a froth of dirt and roots. His knee gives a sudden slide to the left. He nearly goes sailing off the hillside. He has to flatten himself against the rocks to regain his balance. The wall above him is smooth, faceless. He's too short to grip the top edge and, even if he could, not strong enough to hoist himself that high. He tries to climb back down, but the way his leg lashes at the air, slipping short of its foothold, makes his muscles feel like they are floating free of his bones. The others, Kenneth and Thad and Bateman, are already somewhere overhead, flicking long curves of spit onto the grass—gleeking, it's called, and no one has ever been able to teach him how to do it. He can hear the snap of their tongues against their teeth, and then Thad bragging, "Coke bottle!" and Kenneth saying, "Negro, you did *not* hit that," and Bateman beginning his Eddie Murphy routine, powering up his slow, shameless fox's laugh. He stays fastened to the bluff, glancing this way and that, as if the trees or the clouds or the roof of the Shell station could undo the last thirty seconds and give him another chance. It would be just like him, a classic Kevin move, to die here while his friends tell dick jokes.

His throat is so dry that talking seems impossible, but "Guys," he manages to say. "Hey, Thad! Bateman! I need some help."

Thad's head appears, Whack-a-Moling out over the grass. "Having some trouble?"

"How did you guys make it up there?"

"See that big rock? You want to go around the other side."

"I can't. I'm stuck."

"You weigh like seventy-five pounds, man. Here." Thad lets down an arm, and gravity instantly ropes his skin with veins.

Kevin counts to three and releases his fingers from the root fibers of the pine tree. He is ready to fall, ready to break a leg or worse. He is always amazed by the difference between how he feels and how he appears, the way his single-minded determination can look like the panicky darting motion of a little kid.

"Ow," Thad says. "Not my hand, gaybait. Take my wrist," and then there is the same sensation Kevin remembers feeling when he played rocketship in the swimming pool. His body is lofted into the air, and before he knows it, he is lying safe on the ground, bugs the size of celery seeds springing in multitudes out of the clover.

It was last winter when Kevin's dad and stepmom moved to Brandon, Mississippi, a town roughly half the size of its own reservoir. That was where he spent the summer, watching R-rated videos and buying candy from a bait-and-tackle store, playing with his little brother instead of his friends, his head brimming with fantasies of everything he might be missing. Barely a week has passed since he returned to Little Rock. Home to his records and his comics and his room with the big wooden *K* on the door. Home to his friends and their ten thousand changes. Suddenly everyone is saying *badass* rather than *awesome*, *lame* rather than *stupid*, *gaybait* rather than *faggot*, and mostly the gaybait is him. They have taken up a medley of black slang—*holmes*, *boy-ee*, *negro*—pronouncing the words with a strange slingshot rubberiness. Their one-liners are borrowed from *Fletch* now, not *Beverly Hills Cop*, and in their tape players Mötley Crüe has been replaced by Iron Maiden, Dio, and W.A.S.P. And then there are their social lives, that elaborate nervous arrangement of who owns what, who called when, who kissed who and where. In May, Kenneth was going with Sarah, but they split up in July, and now she likes Thad, or at least that's what Jess said. (She certainly doesn't like Kevin.) M.B.'s parents bought a new house in Colony West, and it looks like Carina's are divorcing. Bateman's moped was stolen from his back porch—by Ethan and Kenneth, it turns out—but they returned it that same afternoon. Stephanie is leaving Central Arkansas Christian to attend a secular school, Nathan has moved with his family to Texas, and Greg, who made a *V* of his arms and called out, "Boom time!" whenever he scored a goal during soccer; Greg, who liked to tackle Kevin, clamp his legs around him, and say, "Don't you want to get up? Why don't you get up? Come on, Brockmeier, get up off the ground"—Greg has recruited his older brother to pen Kevin in a locker on the first day of seventh grade, one of the tall athletic models the senior high kids use, and there's not a damn thing he can do about it.

In Arkansas, in August, the sun is so indomitable that the light melts on the pavement, collecting in silver puddles that reflect the sky and split like water around the tires of the cars. Bateman, whose shirt is ribboned with sweat, the cotton clinging transparently to his gut and nipples, says, "This heat is a bitch, mans. Let's get something to drink."

They take the easy route back down the bluff. The sidewalk outside the pizza parlor is so muggy, the foyer so frigid, that goose pimples contour their arms as soon as they step inside. All at once it feels like winter: September, October, November—*whoosh*. An old Pac-Man machine fills the room with its electronic swallowing noise. Absentmindedly, Thad attempts to reproduce the sound: "Huey-huey-huey-huey."

There is a moment of perilous quiet before Kenneth pounces. "Huey-*huey*? What the fuck is huey-*huey*?" Then Kevin says, "It's not huey-huey. He goes waka-waka, doesn't he?" and Bateman says, "I thought it was wookiee-wookiee," and Kevin tries, "Nookie-nookie," and Thad says, "Pussy-pussy," and Kenneth says, "Licky-licky."

They keep running through their variations as they head for the soda fountain. Kevin unzips his backpack and distributes the stack of plastic yellow Mazzio's cups he has been saving. One by one they fill them from the soda spouts. Someone has to cap off the line, and today it is Bateman, which means that he is the one waiting for the foam to settle when the stocky little manager comes tugboating over from the ovens, trailing a pair of skinny waiters behind him. He smacks a hand on the ice bin. "Just what are you boys doing?"

Bateman gives the Coke lever another tap. "These are end-lessly refillable."

"Look, kid, the free refills are for when you order some-thing off the menu. You can't just wander in off the street and start drinking whenever you feel like it."

"It doesn't say that in the commercials."

"It's strongly implied."

"What do you want us to do, dump it out?"

The manager wipes the oil from his brow with a shirt-sleeve. "No—go, go. Drink your Cokes. But don't try this stunt in here again."

November, October, September, and they are back outside, in the heat and the daylight and the damp air with blurred spots of gnats sliding through it. There is a rumor everyone has heard that when the cook scorches a pizza, Mazzio's tosses it in the trash barrel out back, coated with red pepper flakes to keep the homeless from stealing it, but when the four of them investigate, they find only a mound of raw dough the sickish color of something trapped in a swimming pool filter, slowly bloating through the holes in the rusty metal. It is easy for Kevin to imagine it coming to life and terrorizing them. He says, "Beware the Blob," hoping for a laugh, but the alley behind the restaurant is so sticky and unpleasant that the joke frays away before he has quite finished speaking.

The others seem not to hear him. They sit on the wooden ties that divide the hillside from the parking lot and sink the rest of their sodas. Heaped behind them is a clinkery of dis-carded beer bottles. Thad has the idea to line them up for points and aim rocks at them from the top of the bluff. They set to work arranging the bottles in a row, posting them along the tarry wall. Kevin places a green one at the very edge, then smacks the wastewater from a clear one and balances it on top of two browns—a three-pointer.

"Hey, Kevin," Kenneth says. He points to an empty bolt hole in one of the ties. "Here's a question. I'm not making fun of you, I'm just curious: Could you fit your penis in there?"

Kevin inspects Kenneth's face for signs of ridicule, but all he sees is the question, floating there with its beak out like a hummingbird. He decides it is safe to answer. "Not when it's hard, no, but otherwise—I don't know." He slips his finger into the hole. "Maybe it's long enough, but I don't think it's quite wide enough."

In his stomach he feels a wringing sensation, but it comes and it goes and there is no trap waiting for him, no ambush, just his best friends wearing the even-eyed expressions of teachers making checkmarks on a worksheet.

Soon Bateman sets the last bottle in place, and they step back to inspect the display: thirty-some jewels of green, brown, and yellow glass flinging kinks of sunlight out at the afternoon. Kevin decides to give the soul voice a try: "Ahh-ight, boy-ees. I think we got us a contest here." It is a decent effort but not truly convincing. The others say, "I get the first throw," and, "Go to hell, *you get the first throw*. It was my idea," and, "All right, first one to the top then," and begin scaling the bluff. He watches from below as they go Spider-Manning from rock to rock. Then he follows behind them, starting with the trench that reaches along the bottom of the wall and ending with the crumbly dirt ledge an arm's length from the summit. This time he manages to finish the climb without any help, boosting himself onto level ground. Yes. The grass is so tall that the wind seems to scurry through it like a troop of small animals. Kenneth, Thad, and Bateman have already set to work. Kevin rises to his feet and joins them. The soil holds its rocks so tightly that when they pry them loose it makes a sound like burlap tearing. All but the largest fit neatly in the palms of their hands. They offer a perfect quarter-pound of throwing weight, as if they were planted there for just that reason: to send beer bottles tumbling through the air like gymnasts. The bottles pop and they shatter, one after the other, leaving a few jagged cups of glass sitting on the wood. Bateman and Thad are barraging the wall with rocks, trying to demolish the lone survivor, when the manager of Mazzio's comes crunching through the wreckage. "Hey, you little shits, knock it off!"

"Knock what off?"

"You're filling my lot here with glass, that's what."

It is true, the asphalt shines like a mirror beneath him, but what can you do with a day so bright that nearly everything shines like a mirror—the green of the leaves, the brown of the dirt, the gray of the roofs and the pavement?

Thad lets a rock fall *thud* from his hand. "Sir, we are so, so sorry," he says. "We must be total idiots. We didn't realize."

"Yeah, well, stupendous. Magnificent. Me and my people are gonna have to clean this mess up, though, you know? Or else someone'll flatten a tire. Just use your heads from now on."

"We will, sir. And again, we're really sorry. Oh, and one more thing: fuck you, harpy-fucker."

It is one of Thad's favorite cutdowns, borrowed from Kevin's *Monster Manual*—an insult so dirty and inventive that it ticks off nearly everyone who hears it. But the manager just sighs and scuffs back inside, a monkey look of disappointment on his face. It is the expression of someone just like Kevin, with a tendency to believe the best of people until the very last second.

A long moment of insects and car horns passes. A blackbird lands in the crown of an oak tree, caws three times, and flaps away again. Only then do they decide the manager is not returning.

And maybe that counts as a win for them, but if so it is a frustrating one. The dude has taken the possibility of a great story, one they could have shared between them forever, and ruined it by failing to lose his temper. "It's like a bad Fourth of July," Kevin says, thinking of those bottle rockets that go sailing off with a *phrrt* of black powder and vanish into the silence of the sky.

The four of them decide to set off for Kevin's house in case the manager surprises them by calling the police. It is the last weekend of summer, the last weekend before seventh grade, when CAC's three elementary schools braid their twelve-year-olds together with the junior high and high schoolers at the big redbrick building on the hilltop overlooking the river brush. Thad is spending the night with Kevin, and Kenneth is spending the night with Bateman, and tomorrow they will return home to their families and wait for the day to empty out. Then, on Monday, they will all wake up and everything will be different.

On the far side of the field, where the valley rises up to meet the hilltop, is the apartment complex where Miss Moon, their sixth grade teacher, lives. She is tall and slight, with brown hair and blue eyes that seem drained of their color by her freckleless white piano-key skin. Something about the sound of her tongue stumbling over their names when she scolds them fills the boys in Kevin's class with shivers of sexual longing. He has never understood it. She is pretty the way a statue is pretty. Who would turn his eye toward a grown-up when there are girls their own age, impossibly gorgeous girls, who might actually let you touch them someday, and who would let you touch them now if you were touching material? Who would desire anyone else when there is Sarah Bell, Sarah Bell, Sarah Bell—say it loud and listen to it ring—whose fingers grazed Kevin's leg last spring during chapel and made him feel as if his skin had suddenly grown too tight for him?

Kevin is good with stories and always has been. At school, whenever he has finished his work and doesn't feel like borrowing a book from the library or mapping a dungeon out on a sheet of graph paper, he likes to write mystery stories with himself as the detective and his classmates as the kidnap victims—The Case of the Missing Tanla Pickett; The Case of the Missing Ethan Carpenter—or superhero stories that mingle the Marvel Universe together with the DC Universe, or science fiction stories about a motorcyclist named Ace who leads two separate lives, waking into one the instant he falls asleep in the other, or ghost stories with paragraphs that conceal the names of all the shows on prime-time TV. In their group Bateman is the clown, Thad the heartbreaker, Kenneth the cool guy. What is Kevin but the inventor, the storyteller, the negro with the big imagination? It might be the single thing his friends like best about him. And so, as they walk through the apartment complex, he spins a pornographic little what-if for them, pulling this string and that, a fantasy in which one of them—take your pick—disconnects his penis and ships it to Miss Moon in the mail, and "What on earth could this be?" she wonders, flicking its head, tapping it against her palm, holding it distractedly between her teeth, where she chews on it softly like a pencil, pleased and astonished when it begins to change its shape, so that she exclaims, "Oh my goodness, what a fun little toy!" and, "Let's see what else it can do," testing it with her lips and her tongue and her fingers as it transmits its psychic antenna signals across the city, until Kenneth seems to scarecrow-dance out of his limbs and says, "God, God, God, Kevin. Jesus. You have to stop right now."

They pass a slender tree lashed to a triangle of stakes. A nest the size of a tea saucer has toppled out of its branches. Bateman tips it over with his shoe so they can look underneath. There on the grass, spilling out of a speckled blue egg, is the goo of a half-formed bird, a strange lump of Vaseline with a dark net of veins inside it, connecting a pair of eyes and a tweezerlike beak and the popped red balloons of several tiny organs, one of which must be its heart. Kevin can hardly stand to look at it. That this transparent stew of parts, slopping around in the darkness of its shell, is all the bird will ever be gives him an awful gutshot feeling he cannot name, and he knows that if he thinks about it for too long tears will rise to his eyes. He has always been the kid who cries too easily and laughs too easily, the kid who begins giggling in church for no reason at all, who blinks hotly in shame and frustration whenever he misses a question in class, living in an otherland of sparkling daydreams and imaginary catastrophes.

Out of the blue Kenneth says to him, "Hey, Kevin, I'm not making fun of you, I'm just curious: Could you fit your dick in that egg?"

"Shut up."

"Hey, Kevin, I'm not making fun of you, I'm just curious," Thad says. "Do you have any hair on your dick yet?"

"What's you all's obsession with my dick, anyway?"

And then it is Bateman's turn: "Hey, Kevin, what about your balls? Your Tes-ti-clees? Any hair down there?"

"All right. Cut it out, guys."

"We're not making fun of you, we're just curious."

Kevin's house is one snaking downhill street and half an uphill street away. The wind has fallen still, so calm that the clouds appear to be painted onto the sky. The insects have stopped creaking, the trees stopped whisking the air with their fingertips. By the time they reach his carport, all four of them look like Bateman, their shirts glued to their shoulders with sweat. Kevin goes to the refrigerator for a Little Hug, an orange one. He peels the foil cap off the plastic barrel and stands there chugging the drink, his hand on the open door. This time it is December in front of him and August behind. The refrigerator wicks the moisture from his chest and stomach. "Ah, *mans*, this feels good," he says, and before long Thad, Bateman, and Kenneth are clustered with him in the light of the refrigerator, like campers bunched around a fire, washing down Little Hugs. It is almost 3:30—snack time. But when Kevin makes the announcement, the others laugh and say, "*Snack* time?" and "Hey, it's *time* for *snacks*, everyone," and "Holmes, I don't know a single other house that does that. Only yours," until the drums in his head go click-click-click and snack time is safely stored away, added to the list of things it is impermissible to acknowledge or say.

His brother, Jeff, is spending the night somewhere else,

with Jack Barnard or Jason Burton probably, his unknowable separate friends from his unknowable separate life, which means that until Kevin's mom gets home from work, the house is entirely theirs. They are the grown-ups and can eat whatever they want, in whichever room they choose. They sling their bodies across the couch and the loveseat, trading a box of Cheez-Its back and forth. Shortly before dinner, Kenneth climbs onto the bumper seat of Bateman's moped, and the two of them go putting out of the driveway, and have you ever noticed how, from a distance, a moped can sound like a bird rattling out a message in the trees? Soon Kevin's mom arrives home with Happy Meals from McDonald's. Thad and Kevin eat their cheeseburgers and fries at the kitchen counter, sitting on the tall wooden stools with the vinyl cushions, leaning slowly over until they have steadied themselves on the two side legs, then pivoting onto the two back ones. They are trapeze artists. Acrobats. They spend the rest of the night booting the soccer ball around the backyard and walking to the gas station for candy and eventually, after Kevin's mom has shut her door and they have given her almost an hour to fall asleep, trying to distinguish the breasts from the scramble waves in the blue-green go-anywhere of the Playboy Channel, all sound and no picture.

It is after midnight before they turn out the lights. Kevin lies down in bed, Thad on the floor in his sleeping bag. From out of the darkness Thad asks, "So are you ready for school? My mom and dad let me use my birthday money to buy this gold chain I'm gonna wear around my neck. Herringbone."

"Here's the thing," Kevin announces. "Greg and his brother better stay the hell away from me, that's all I have to say. I'll tell the principal on them if I have to. I'll do it. Watch me."

"Uh-huh. You know, Greg's brother isn't really going to stuff you in a locker. He's gone—Greg and his brother both are. They moved away in July. We just told you that 'cause we wanted to see if you would freak out. You freaked out, didn't you?"

Kevin would like to kick the sheets off his bed, would like them to plummet to the carpet like a missile. "A little."

"I knew it. We were all—I don't know, not *annoyed* with you really. We just wanted to screw with your head. It started when you sent us those sneaker stickers this summer. That's when we came up with the locker story. I can't explain it. They were so weird and random. It was like, *Thanks but what the fuck? Sneakers?* Why did you mail us those?"

"I thought you guys would like them."

He remembers buying the stickers from the greeting card aisle of the Jitney Jungle when his dad took him grocery shopping. His only other choices were rainbows, ladybugs, or dogs with American flag bandannas. For the second time that day, Kevin feels a clutching in his throat, the salt sting of tears in his eyes. No. He is trying hard not to be him anymore, that kid.

Sometimes, huddled in his sleeping bag, Thad can be unexpectedly nice, saying things like, "Well, it's the thought that counts. You know, it's all cool. But everyone is done collecting stickers—finished—so don't go giving us any more. And nothing involving shoes, either. In fact, maybe you should just stop buying people presents all the time. None of that shit at all. So are you nervous? I can't believe that two days from now we'll be in junior high."

"One-point-five."

"Yeah, I'm going to wear my gold chain. Kenneth met some

of the Sylvan Hills and Geyer Springers at football practice. He says they're not too bad. I saw this blond chick when I went to register, and she was totally hot. I mean, Jesus Christ the shape of her ass. Like two scoops of ice cream in a glass bowl. You wouldn't believe it. So are you nervous?"

In kindergarten, when they were little, he and Thad used to play *Star Wars* on the jungle gym during recess, one of them the morning Han Solo, the other the afternoon. In third grade, they told elaborate lies during show-and-tell, Thad inventing Scooby-Doo stories about his dog Clarence, a coward and a mischief-maker, while Kevin reported the dreams he pretended to remember from the night before. Once, in fifth grade, the two of them showed their middle fingers to a whole squad of teenagers at the State Fair, escaping through the midway by the barest slip of space. And last year, nearly every Friday night, they met up with Kenneth and Bateman and a few of the others at Eight Wheels, where the younger kids skated the blue-lit oval of the wooden rink while the older kids stood around flirting in their high-tops. It was Kevin's job, each week toward nine o'clock, to run out front and intercept whichever parent had agreed to fetch them while Kenneth and Thad finished making out with their girlfriends behind the building.

"Honestly, I just don't want anything to change."

"Me either," says Thad.

"I'm sick of things being different all the time."

"Me too."

And then it happens again, the same way it has happened a hundred times before, with the gaps between their answers growing longer and longer until their voices can barely leap over the stillness. Soon neither of them quite remembers what the other has said or whose turn it is to speak. Kevin is swooning into a dream of girls and dark rooms when his leg twitches and wakes him back up. A car goes roaring down the street toward the cowboy bar. Its headlights brighten the window. Then the glass seems to hitch in its frame, and the brightness pops loose, curving and flashing across the ceiling before it vanishes behind the dresser. He has missed his chance, his one chance, to dive through it and find out where it would have taken him. He turns onto his left side, his sleeping side, and lies there listening to the whoosh of the air conditioner. The day keeps coming to light again in bits and pieces: the jellyfish-like burst of the pine tree letting go of the hillside, and the sound of bottles shattering on the asphalt, and Tes-ti-clees the ancient Greek god, and suicides of Coke and Sunkist and Dr Pepper, and the poor bird draining from its egg into the grass, and the tingle of his sweat cooling in a humming rectangle of air, and who liked him and how much and why? One by one his thoughts flow from their outlines like a cloud, and then the cloud rolls over him and he is asleep.

Sunday passes as it always does, with church and Wyatt's Cafeteria and the slow TV hours of the afternoon. Then it is Monday, and his mom is driving him across the river into the trees, and as they crest the hill and coast into the parking lot, the school grows gigantic in the windshield. They pull to a stop at the entrance. Something like a bird shoots out of his heart. Then he steps out onto the patio and becomes a part of it all. The blue sky and the glass doors and the white tile floor that blazes in the sunlight. The lockers crashing shut like cymbals. The high school guys punching each other's shoulders, drafts of cologne and deodorant mixing between their bodies. The high school girls with their hair belled out around their necks. The black streaks of tennis shoe rubber on the floor of the gymnasium. The glass walls of the front office. The Reeboks and Levi's, Izods and bomber jackets, jelly bracelets and Swatch watches. The football players in their jerseys. The band kids with their instrument cases. The chalkboards with their eraser-shaped smoke signals—*poof, poof, poof.* The pay phones in the foyer where the popular girls wait for the first bell to ring. The concession stand with its rolling metal gate. The stairwell with its stack of folding chairs. The couples kissing behind the doors of their lockers, pretending that no one can see them. The chopping and rolling noise of five hundred conversations happening all at once, like a river relaxing along its banks and then plunging ahead, over and over again. The butcher paper banners reading "WELCOME TO MUSTANG MOUNTAIN" and "STAYIN' ALIVE IN 85" in gold and purple, the school colors, which are everywhere, everywhere. The vending machines with their coils of chips and candy. The desks with their attached chairs. The long hallways of open classroom doors, their doorstops like curving brass hoofs. The coaches and the teachers, the principal and the guidance counselor, the janitor in his plaid shirt and dark glasses. The other students, all of them older and bigger, standing in clusters against the walls and the lockers, their eyes sliding past the seventh-graders as they look for their buddies, their teammates, for their girlfriends and boyfriends, for someone who knows them, someone they recognize.

· · · · · · · · · · · · · · · ·

The gym stands on one side of the hall, Mr. Garland's class on the other, and every day, after first period, the girls finishing PE and the boys finishing Bible meet in the middle, twisting around each other like the tails of two kites. Sometimes, if Kevin paces himself just right, he will fall into step with Sarah Bell and her friends—the lip-gloss girls—with brush furrows in their wet hair and Guess triangles on their jeans. He basks in their incense of sweat and shampoo, thinking, This will be the day, the day I tell her a joke and graze her arm, a throwaway touch with the back sides of my fingers, nothing much, just quick and cool, as if I don't care, but then a locker slams shut or a voice cuts through the air and once again the tiny comforting thought caresses his mind: Tomorrow. You can be brave tomorrow.

The high school is all noise and unrest, as different as can be from the churchlike hush of the elementary school. Between periods the building fills with people shouting and running and flicking each other's knuckles with pencils, with choir kids singing, photographers snapping pictures, drill-teamers cocking their hips, with couples bending hard into each other's bodies. In class, they all become the quietest possible versions of themselves, but in the hallways everyone is either a swerver or a strider. The swervers move this way and that, leaning and swaying like tops, taking the quickest route possible through the obstacle course of other people's bodies, while the striders choose a single path and follow it like a marble rolling down a chute. Kevin is a born swerver. He likes the sensation of bobbing beneath someone's upraised arm, slipping sideways past a big clump of juniors and seniors, that wonderful feeling of swiftness and intangibility. No one can catch him, no one can touch him. He could be a ghost rushing through a brick wall, a motocross racer, almost anything.

One day, just before the end of first period, the chemistry teacher, Mr. Shoaf, seeds the corridor outside his room with sulfur pellets, hundreds of little yellow beads that pop open with the earthy stink of rotten eggs. The odor washes through the northern wing of the school, and after the bell, as the boys in Kevin's class step into the hallway, their faces take on the startled looks of sunbathers doused in cold water. They cough theatrically or give bewildered laughs. They tack their hips to the side as if they've cut a fart. Sarah, walking just ahead of them in her denim skirt and white ankle socks, says, "Barf," and tugs the collar of her shirt up over her nose to mask the smell. That mouth, those breasts—Kevin wants to make a little bed between them.

"Shit, man," Levon Dollard says, taking an instinctive whiff. "This place fucking reeks."

And *ting!*—That's what you get when the girls take PE, Kevin thinks.

There is funny ha-ha, and there is funny peculiar, and beneath a trapdoor in Kevin's mind is a place where the two blur together, the place of jokes, churning so furiously that frequently, when it kicks up a line, he has no idea what it will turn out to be. He has discovered that whether a joke is truly witty doesn't matter—only the glow in his voice, the glitter of invention. But Levon is one of the new kids, from Sylvan Hills or Geyer Springs, a tall ropy football player who isn't familiar enough with Kevin to take it for granted that he is funny, so he bungles the delivery. "The girls. PE. You know, all that sweat."

No one laughs. It is funny embarrassing.

Then Jess Watts says, "Or maybe it's your upper lip, Kevin Brockmeier," which everyone finds hilarious.

Kevin is baffled. He understands the implication, that he is the one who stinks, *he who smelt it dealt it*—but his upper lip? Why? Surreptitiously, he runs his fingers over his mouth, but they come back clean, smelling of soap, pencil lead, and the leather strap of the camera satchel he uses for a book bag. Nothing disgusting.

On the staircase landing, he calls out to M.B., who answers, "What did I say? I'm going by *Michael* now. Write it down. *Michael*."

"Whatever. Hey, do you see anything on my upper lip?"

"Like your nose?"

"Yes. Exactly. Like my nose. Very helpful, M.B."

"No problemo."

The intercom makes its electronic bell sound, a shrill tone with a strange dust of static at the beginning, and they hurry into their classes. In English, Miss Vincent fills the left side of the chalkboard with adjectives, then asks them to add their own words to the list: "Give me five adjectives— five attributes—you would use to describe yourself to a

stranger." Kevin is (1) scrawny, (2) oversensitive, (3) unath-
letic, (4) mouselike, and (5) girlfriendless. No, no, he is (1)
friendly, (2) clever, (3) imaginative, and (4) likable. He is (5)
awesome-beyond-all-adjectives. He is a good student, a fast
writer. He charges through his assignments like a runner
sprinting down a track, then sits at his desk daydreaming or
reading novels, making up stories or mapping out dungeons.

For the rest of the day, in Coach Dale's geography class,
Mrs. Dial's math class, Mrs. Bissard's SRA class—and why
don't they just call it *reading*?—he fills his spare time puz-
zling through Jess's wisecrack. Either she just chose a part
of his body at random, or there is something special about his
upper lip, something he can't figure out. The question, then,
is what makes his upper lip unique? He has noticed that it
has a tiny discoloration just off-center, soft and pale, like a
cut immediately after it has finished healing, but how would
Jess have seen that? He spotted it only a few nights ago himself, and solely by chance, studying his face in the bathroom
mirror to see if he could make his tongue ripple. What else?
His upper lip is pink and slender, much thinner than his
lower lip. It is shaped like a bird in a landscape painting, that
bowlike symbol preschoolers learn with their very first box of
watercolors: an *M* with its legs pulled flat. In the winter sometimes, when he forgets to wear ChapStick, the skin above his
lips becomes so red that it looks like the stain from a cherry
popsicle—but that's in January and February, not the second
week of September. Brother. His ideas are getting less complicated by the minute. Let's see: his upper lip is above his chin
and beneath his nose. It is part of his mouth. He talks with his
mouth, he sings with his mouth, he eats with his mouth, he

drinks with his mouth. He uses his mouth to smile, to pout, to whistle, to yawn, to spit, to breathe, and to kiss. And that, he finally decides, is it. His upper lip or his lower lip, it makes no difference—he uses them, uses them both, to kiss.

Jess's putdown meant that he had kissed something repulsive. He is an ass-kisser—that's what she was saying.

He feels the satisfaction of cracking the code, a fine warm body-lightness that causes his fingers and toes to tingle. Simultaneously, though, he can't help but wonder: Is Jess right? Is he an ass-kisser, a suck-up? And how would he know if he was? The truth is he spends thirty minutes of every hour suspecting he has missed some essential clue about himself. And not only himself—he has a recurring fantasy that one night, while he was asleep, the entire world was transformed into an alien planet, but no one bothered to tell him, and he didn't have the instinct to figure it out, and here he is now on a wild new Earth, walking around like an imbecile, as if everything he knows hasn't fallen away behind him like a river plummeting over a precipice.

At 3:30, the final bell rings. He returns to his homeroom to collect the overnight bag containing his clothes and his toiletries. Then he follows the crowd to the buses centipeding across the parking lot, a half dozen idling old athletic vehicles, their yolky orange color faded by the sunlight.

It is a golden Friday afternoon, the very last minute of the school week, and for a moment he simply stands there at the edge of the weekend. The days and nights make a quiet sound of possibility, rustling and ticking like a dark forest. The campground at Lake Bennett, forty miles up the highway, is hosting a sleepaway for everyone at CAC, seventh-graders through seniors, permission slips required. Who knows what could happen between now and Monday morning?

The teachers are busy directing people to their assigned buses: *Eighth grade, I'm looking for the eighth grade! Yo, SOPH-mores! Juniors right here—come on, folks, let's get a move on!* Thad, Kenneth, and Bateman have already packed themselves into the long bench at the back of the seventh-grade bus, along with a couple of new kids, Shane Roper and Joseph Rimmer, who seem to Kevin like the same shaggy, drowsy cutup ladled into two separate bodies, one brown-haired and the other blond, both of them laughing all the time at some private joke they've exchanged with a twitch of their eyebrows. Thad says to Kevin, "Sorry, neeg-bo, no room in the rear for you," and in his dirtiest voice Shane repeats, "In the rear," and Joseph says, "Up the butt," and Kenneth says, "Holmes, did you just call dude *neeg-bo*?" and the word echoes against the walls as Kevin walks away: *neeg-bo, neeg-bo, neeg-bo.*

He finds a seat next to Ethan, one of the three Carpenters in their class, just as Sarah is one of the three Bells, Thad one of the three Brookses, Jennifer one of the two Grahams. Kevin is the only Brockmeier.

He and Ethan Carpenter are Billy Joel friends, comic book friends. Together they have made countless Saturday afternoon expeditions to Gadzooks, a small fluorescent box of a store that smells of Windex and carpet glue, as if the desks and filing cabinets of some one-room insurance office had been replaced with glass cabinets full of vintage toys and racks of the latest Marvels and DCs. The two of them spend the ride talking superheroes, arguing which-is-better-and-why. The Avengers or the Justice League? Batman or Wolverine? They both agree: the Punisher.

Soon the lakeshine pierces the trees, and the road hooks down through the grass, and the bus comes crunching to a stop in the wet sand. The door folds open, and everyone stands up to leave, pressing and bunching down the aisle. Mr. McCallum, the principal, waits in the courtyard in his tie and short-sleeved shirt, his thin hair whipped up from his scalp by the breeze. He looks like a baseball player dressed uncomfortably for church, addressing them as "guys and gals," and saying, "Grab your gear and choose a bunk. Boys to the left and girls to the right. Hot dogs are at six o'clock, lights out at eleven. Otherwise have fun and don't drown in the lake."

Kevin's is the last bag unloaded from the cargo bin. He wants to sleep next to Thad, and if not Thad then Kenneth or Bateman, but by the time he reaches the building, all the beds have been taken. The only empty bunk he can find is in a private suite on the far side of the barracks. It is a prize room, easily the best in the lodge, with a window, a table, a couch, and a dresser, and though it is already being shared by three ninth-graders he recognizes from his elementary school days—that world without end of chapels and lunches, kickball matches and recesses, amen, amen—no one stops him from claiming the remaining bed. Before long the ninth-graders head out for the docks to borrow a canoe, and a short while later, four grown seniors come charging in to gorilla-toss their bags into the hallway. Kevin lies on his stomach reading a Two-Minute Mystery while they tramp around the room claiming mattresses, kicking the sand off their shoes, and stuffing their clothes in the dresser—all but the big one, who stands watching the mayhem from the shoulder of the couch. Then Kevin is alone again.

"Say hey, man, let me chat with you a second." An older kid

is leaning in the doorway, all black jeans and catlike posing. "I'm Rory. You?"

My name is Kevin Brockmeier; I collect *What If*s and *X-Men*; my favorite band is New Edition.

"Kevin."

"Awesome. So listen. The big guy who was just in here? That's David Henson. He's out there feeling like you've robbed him of his bed. He was All-Conference last year, as a *junior*. I'm talking the Razorbacks have their eyes on him. Now I know you got here first, but there's another room just down the hall. Three beds instead of four—that's the only difference. You can get a couple of buds and take that one instead. Sound good?"

"I guess so."

"Cool. Give me two names, and I'll tell them where to meet you."

One: Thad; and two: Bateman—Kevin doesn't hesitate. He is like a gymnast of favorites, keeping his muscles limber and his reflexes honed by asking himself again and again, at every opportunity, which songs he prefers, which girls he likes, who his best friends are. Kenneth is number three today. Kevin hopes his feelings won't be hurt. He half-suspects the other room is a scam, anyway, an invention, and he'll end up sleeping on the bus or sharing a mattress with Jim Boothby, one of the few kids at CAC, boy or girl, who is smaller than he is. But the room is real, with one cabin bed and one bunk bed and a fan that spins so hard it makes the ceiling light totter. Kevin is thumping the seat of a chair stretched with army canvas when the Rory guy raps on the doorframe. "Well, Kev, looks like you lucked out. Those friends of yours have already dug in for the weekend."

"Kenneth wasn't ticked off, was he? You said only two people. That was the precondition. If he's ticked off, then maybe he can trade with Bateman tomorrow night?"

"No, man, look, you didn't hear me. Nobody's coming. You've got this place all to yourself."

That night, at lights out, after a cookout that shoots coal sparks into the sandy grass and a hayride where Carina DeCiccio lets the round part of her hip rest against him, Kevin lies quietly in the gray darkness, listening to the fan whir the way a cricket chirps.

Saturday he wakes later than usual. The men's room has already emptied out. Beneath the open row of shower nozzles are only a bottle of Prell and a few slick patches of concrete, and he is able to wash himself without embarrassment. The noises outside the lodge are sliced off by the rush of the water. As soon as he closes the tap, though, they resume. The hull of a motorboat smacking the surface of the lake. A softball *wha-rack*ing against a bat. A group of footballers goofing around like cheerleaders, Weird Al–ing their way through the Mustang Spirit chant: *ah-lean, lean, ah-lean-lean-lean-lean.*

Kevin towels himself off and dresses. He is using the toilet when the bathroom door creaks open, and all at once it's, "Whoof," and, "Jesus Christ, do you smell that?" and, "Do I *smell* that? Of *course* I smell that. Dude's been eating *road-kill*, and you ask me if I smell that." Then someone must peer beneath the stall because Kevin hears a voice whisper, "Check it out—shoes," and he understands that they are talking about him.

After a while, he has no choice but to rise and zip, buckle and flush. He opens the stall door. Three upperclassmen, sturdy Roman pillar types, are standing quietly by the hot-air blower, waiting with their arms crossed. The moment they see Kevin and his little straw body they lose it. Laughter blooms from their mouths like a chain of musical notes, dozens of tiny stems and noteheads popping open and ringing off the walls. The three of them cling, gasping, to one another's shoulders, and stumble against the sink counter. Kevin watches their fingers shape miniature invisible boxes in the air, a gesture some of the older girls have carried into the school from their summers, meaning *how small, how cute, look at the teensy-weensy adorable little baby.*

He can't help it—he starts grinning along with them. He is not just some jerk in a story. He is in on the joke.

It takes him forty minutes of roaming through the park to locate his friends. Along the curve of the lake is a thick place of oaks where the light that strains through the leaves meets the light that dances off the water, playing over his skin in hundreds of greenish gold threads. Beyond the docks is a chain of boathouses where gray squirrels sprint *tik-tik-tik* over the tin roofs. They bound across the gaps without a second's pause, sailing in a frozen stretch, like runners leaping hurdles, before they land and unlock and keep running.

Kevin's mind won't stop replaying the incident in the bathroom. If you ask him, the whole thing wasn't half as funny as those other guys thought it was. What was the punch line supposed to be? Big things come in small packages? Hilarity.

He wishes he had been quick enough to produce a comeback, some sterling silver one-liner he could have dropped at their feet like a coin.

Blank—that's what he should have said.

This.

Whatever it was, it would have been perfect.

The more he thinks about it, the more embarrassed he becomes. All the same, when he passes the picnic table where the older kids are sitting with their buddies and hears, "There he is. That's him. The Source," he experiences a queer proud sensation of minor fame. They have given him a name. The hair on the back of his neck prickles. He hopes they haven't told that Rory guy.

Eventually he catches the rhythm of Bateman repeating his favorite baby story, the one about the time he scraped his knee playing in front of his house. Kevin can recognize it by the beats alone:

"I fall down."
Where did you fall down?
"In the street."
WHAT were you doing in the street?
"Falling down."

He cuts around the wall of a pavilion and finds the usual gang standing in a patch of grass-stitched dirt. He hiked past the spot not five minutes ago, and it was completely deserted. "Jeez, bros," he says. "I've been to Conway and back practically. Where did you all migrate in from?"

"We've been around."

"Here and there."

"Mass murdering."

This from Shane Wesson, who never says something true if he can say something ridiculous. But Shane begins stamping the ground, planting his foot flat and firm like elephants do, and Kevin realizes that he is referring to what Mr. Garland told them one day in science class—how with every step you take, thousands of minuscule creatures are crushed beneath your weight. "To the grave! Die, foul microorganisms!"

Kenneth says, "All right already, Shane. It's getting lame. Ell-ay-*ame*." Then Bateman says, "It's way past lame, it's mame," and Clint Fulkerson, a tall kid with white jeans and straight bangs and a weirdly handsome science fiction face, like a *Tiger Beat* Spock, says, "Yeah, dude, enough with the microorganisms," and Bateman dives back in with, "By now it's nearly name," and Kevin seals his palms over his ears and says, "La la la."

Something happens in Thad's expression, like a knife sharpening against a stone. "La la *la*? What the fuck is la la *la*?"

"It's like, cut it out. You know, like, I don't want to hear it."

Thad parrots him syllable for syllable, replacing all the words he used with *la*'s. "La *la*, la la la. La la, la, la *la* la la *la* la."

Kenneth and Bateman, Joseph and Clint, Shane Roper and Shane Wesson—for a while it is a concert of *la*'s, all of them talking at once. There is a problem with Kevin's eyes again. He reddens and blinks, looking away so that no one will notice. By his shoe lies a bottle cap—the prying kind, not the twisting kind—with a flat clot of dirt inside it. It could be a pie tin for Smurfs or Littles. He kicks it and watches it slide off toward the trees. He wishes some distraction would come along and conceal him from everyone. A bomb. A tornado. And soon enough a cute eighth-grader, Dana Tread-way, strolls by with her friends. Thad and Kenneth shout

out "Dana Banana" until she reaches the door of the snack bar, where she wheels around and gives them a big bracey escape-smile. Then it's, "Dang, did you see that?" and, "She wants you, holmes. She totally wants you," and Kevin feels like Moses or Daniel, Houdini or David Copperfield, allowed by some miracle to slip out of his chains.

Seemingly overnight, his friends have discovered a new method of spitting, and he looks on as they show off their technique. Here's how it works: you stroke your throat for a while, then gasp as if you are fumbling a stack of plates—*Aw-ah! Oh God! Here it comes!*—varying it up sometimes by adding a girl's name, until you are ready to throw your head back and fire off a pearl of spit. It looks easy enough, but try as he might, Kevin can't quite get it right, and after three or four attempts, he quietly gives up. He has never been any good at these games. It seems smarter just to stand back and watch, to let his friends take turns priming their throats and spotting the ground with saliva, to laugh when he senses he is supposed to laugh, swear when he senses he is supposed to swear.

He slept through breakfast and missed his usual snack time, so by 1:15, when the lunch bell calls everyone to the courtyard—a lunch horn, actually, three quick taps from one of the buses—he is literally starving. No, Kevin, the Miss Vincent in his head corrects him: Not *literally*. You're *figuratively* starving. You're *practically* starving. "This is *literally* the most creative story anyone has ever handed in to me. Your penmanship is *practically* beastly."

He walks with the others back to the lodge, where the teachers have laid out pizzas on folding tables. He can taste the brine of the pepperoni, the ash of the crust, from a good fifty feet away. Cavalcades of gnats and flies follow the smell. Nearby a rope chimes against a flagpole. The girl who steps in line behind him says, "Hey!" and then, "Kevin!" and then, "This is my sister, Lynn. Lynn, this is Kevin. Kevin's the one who's always using the big words in class."

He is? Kevin picks through his memory for the biggest word he knows. The searching expression on his face must look like mystification to the girl, because she says, "You don't remember my name, do you?"

"I was trying to think of a big word to impress you. *Incorrigible.*"

"That's okay. You don't have to be embarrassed. I'm Melissa."

"I'm Kevin. *Absquatulate.*"

She makes a no-kidding gesture. "I just introduced you. By name, remember?"

"Sorry. A reflex."

"So are you like constantly reading books or what?"

He is talking to a girl, and there are a hundred possible answers to her question, but at last he selects the true one: "Pretty much."

"I like that," she says. And then they arrive at the front of the line, where the table splits their conversation down the middle. She and her sister load up their plates with slices of pepperoni, and Kevin takes his usual, two plain slices of cheese. They meet again by the ranks of Cokes, where he says, "Well, bye, then," and Melissa says, "See ya in class," and as the flies make crumb-passes over their plates, they leave to join their separate friends.

Maybe this counts, he thinks.

Maybe something has happened.

Late that afternoon, Kevin and Clay, one of the other Carpenters, borrow a paddleboat and steer it out onto the lake.
Kevin finds himself listening to the soft parting noise the wheel
makes as it dips and surfaces, again and again—a kissing
sound: *pwah pwah pwah pwah*. He has never operated such
a contraption before. There is a dinky toy-car feeling to it.
It's fun, he has to admit, but also kind of ridiculous. He can't
believe that grown-ups do it, too—grown-ups!—with their big
legs and their beer coolers and their sunglasses, pumping and
splishing across the water while Jet Skis and motorboats slice
past them like knives moving through a cake. He and Clay
aim for a clearing on the far side of the nature trail. Every so
often they observe a fish rolling up from the depths. To Kevin
they look like loose pieces of something larger, the gray or
brown forearm of some strange underwater man stretching
slowly up out of the muck, but Clay is able to identify every
one with a single word. "Flathead. Largemouth. Spotted.
Drum." The names are so unlikely that Kevin has a hard time
believing he isn't making them up.

They are pedaling past a knot of trees when they become
aware of two girls quarreling with each other on the shore.
One says, "That's not what you promised me," and the other,
"I already told you. It wasn't my decision, it was Jennifer's,"
and the first again, "Jennifer, my ass. This is totally humiliating for me, don't you get that?" and he knows that it is Sarah
because he knows.

The argument grows louder as the cove angles into sight.
As soon as their boat putters past the trees, Clay spots the
girls and points them out—Sarah and Jess, standing chest to
shoulder by the struts of a wooden dock.

"Jess," Sarah begs. Then she says it again as if it were a command: "Jess. Look. I already *told* everyone. You-know-*who* is going to be there. For once in your life, can't you have a little compassion?"

"It's out of my hands, I'm sorry."

"What, do you want me to say *please*? Okay—please."

"Sugar, you're not getting the picture."

The boat is sliding past so quietly that neither of the girls has noticed it. "You know what? Fuck you," Sarah says, and Jess tosses back the newest answer, which is, "Fuck yourself, save a quarter, this machine is out of order." Then she pivots around and marches away.

"Fine, then!" Sarah yells. Her body makes a fluttering little inhalation, as if the back of her hand has glanced against a hot iron. "Oh come on! And now I bit my lip!" and she launches a kick at one of the dock pilings.

It is the last thing Kevin sees before the water takes her away from him, and the sun emerges from behind a cloud, and the laketop is transformed into a million dots of white confetti.

It is too warm for a bonfire, but that night, after sunset, the seniors are allowed to build one anyway, a small, square box of logs and newspapers that burns at a slant because of the wind, turning white on the lake side and black on the land side. The spectacle of the sparks chasing each other through the air draws half the students in school to the fire. At first they just stand around mesmerized by the light fletching through the logs, their bodies leaning toward the flames, their faces wincing slightly at each explosion of sap, but then Coach Dale leads them in a handful of hymns, "Stand Up and Shout It" and "Teach Me, Lord, to Wait," "Seek Ye First" and

"Kum Ba Yah," and afterward, as a gag, someone strikes up the Christmas carol from *The Grinch*, "Fah who foraze, Dah who doraze," and what could it be but a kind of enchantment that makes everyone bump around and sway, singing along before the whole tune falls apart in laughter?

Right now, Kevin's mom must be waiting for her toenails to dry, the polish saturating her bedroom with its fumes. His brother must be sitting on the living room floor watching the last few minutes of *Airwolf*, eating honey-roasted peanuts out of a Dixie cup on a marble coaster. Percy, their cat, must be lying on top of the TV, making occasional blacked-out sighs as he absorbs the heat from the cable box.

A scrap of newspaper lifts off from the fire, its colors burned inside out, so that the background paper is as dark as coal and the letters are a scorched silver. It floats around for a while, then goes kiting off to the other side of the semicircle. Kevin watches it touch down on one of the older kids from the bathroom.

Blank. Now. This. Here. There.

He still can't decide what he should have said to them.

Gradually the fire sinks in on itself. The embers give off a drowsy orange glow, the kind that reminds him of a railroad crossing, blinking this-side-that-side, this-side-that-side. He is returning to the lodge when it comes to him finally, the ideal comeback.

Or maybe it's your upper lip.

He imagines himself saying it out loud and smiles. He can almost hear the response, an admiring chorus of *damn*'s and *cold*'s and *bro, you got blistered*'s. No doubt about it—it would have made an excellent impression.

By the time he reaches his room, the thrill of the joke is gone. He is changing into his sleeping shirt—FRITZBUSTERS—when a blur drifts over his eyes. He feels himself smacking hard up against his fatigue. He barely has the energy to finish putting himself to bed, but once he does he finds that he is too exhausted to relax. His mind is still full of noise and commotion, a rolling white wave of hyperactivity. Usually, on nights like this, he will lull himself to sleep with a sexual fantasy. Some days, midway through the afternoon, he will concoct one so promising that he will save it up for hours, waiting until he has turned out the lights and reeled off his Our Fathers to deploy it. And here's the thing: no matter how tantalizing the stories he invents, he can never quite seize hold of them. They sheer and whirl and drop from sight like a puff of feathers riding a breeze. He finds it terrifically soothing. How many times has he lain in bed thinking of Sarah, his erection tightening and softening as his mind wanders this way and that? He cannot say. But summoning her up after overhearing her argument with Jess feels disloyal to her somehow, to the way she kicked so stiffly at the dock, like someone who had never kicked anything larger than a dandelion. Instead he pictures himself with Meredith Hopps, a girl he barely knows and does not love, imagining the two of them pressed together in the darkness, playing with each other's nakedness through their clothing.

A chilly lunchtime in mid-October, and Shane Wesson is pinching the head off a blade of foxtail grass. "Hey, you want to see something? Here, put this in your mouth."

Kevin lays the foxtail on the centerline of his tongue. "Now what?" He has scarcely spoken before the prickle of fuzz picks up the tremor and starts crawling toward the back of his throat. He coughs and gags, nipping at it with his teeth, but the more he chases after it, the more quickly it flees. Soon he has no choice but to swallow. He can feel the thing scratching its way down his windpipe like a cylinder of twitching bug's legs.

Shane leans forward, giving his big batty laugh. "It's like it turns into a caterpillar, am I right?"

"It stings!" *Tunk, tunk*—Kevin smacks his breastbone. "It stings right here. Jesus shit, man, what's wrong with you?"

Shane shrugs. "If you reverse it when you put it in, it'll crawl the other way. Nobody ever reverses it, though. People just plant it on their tongue like gardeners or something."

Already it is a quarter past noon. Lunch is nearly over. Between the first and second bell, Kevin stands by the upstairs restroom monopolizing the drinking fountain, taking one huge gulp after another as he tries to wash the foxtail down.

Shane! The guy is a total prick. The guy has a serious problem. He tells lies, and he spills secrets, and he likes to hyperventilate himself, folding his torso over and gasping like a long-distance runner, then snapping upright so that a million sparks cascade through his head. He does it all the time. He's probably damaged that asshole brain of his.

Thinking about the spike of grass shedding its seeds inside him makes Kevin feel sick to his stomach. For the rest of the day the weedy taste lingers in his mouth, thinning out and then intensifying, as if he is walking through his neighborhood on one of those sunny spring Saturdays that lifts all the moisture from the grass, tweezing dandelions through the soil and sending fleets of gas mowers out onto the lawns. Is he just imagining it? He doesn't think so. He keeps showering his tongue with sprays of peppermint Binaca—a new thing: like a handful of Tic Tacs—until finally, in SRA, Mrs. Bissard says, "Who's doing that? Your hair looks fine, girls. Quit primping."

That evening, at home, during a block of commercials, Kevin goes to the bathroom to investigate the inside of his mouth. As far as he can tell, the foxtail has come and gone without leaving a mark. At first he is standing at the mirror with his face spread out around his lips. Then a gear seems to turn, and he is standing at the mirror with his face spread out around his lips *noticing* himself. His bulbous canines. The pinpricks of his freckles. He has a fantasy dating back to preschool that all the mirrors in his house are secretly windows, magic spyglasses for the girls in his class. How often has he pictured them somewhere, at their sinks or by their vanities, casting their girl-spells and peeking in on him? How often has he imagined them gazing through the polished silver squares and ovals on his walls as he combs his hair or changes his clothes or darts down the hall on his way to the refrigerator? And why? Why would they do it? Sometimes, stepping out of the shower, Kevin will catch sight of his reflection and shy off to one side. He embarrasses him, that kid, slouching around with his budlike penis, with his thin chest ridged like the roof of a dog's mouth. He doesn't want anyone looking at him.

Cheers drifts to an end, its last tired piano notes wrapping an inexplicable golden sadness in their hands, and then he hears the air pocket of perfect silence that always announces the beginning of the next program—which on Thursday nights, on NBC, at 8:30, is *Night Court*. He bounds past the chain of empty bedrooms—one two three, Mom's and Jeff's and Kevin's, lined up like dice in a dice box and reclaims his spot on the living room carpet. In this world there are *Cosby Show* people, *Family Ties* people, *Cheers* people, and *Night Court* people. Kevin's friends are more important to him than his family, which rules out *Family Ties*, and also rules out *The Cosby Show*, and he prefers bright rooms to dark rooms, soda to beer, and nearly anyone else in the world to Shelley Long, which rules out *Cheers*. He is a *Night Court* person: quick-thinking, whimsical, bizarre. He likes to stay up late: *Night Court*. His hair is a fiasco: *Night Court*. And he is actually funny: *Night Court*. His favorite character on TV is Bull the bailiff, his favorite video a-ha's "Take On Me," his favorite commercial "Parts Is Parts." His best friend is Thad and sometimes Bateman. He can't wait for the State Fair, which starts this weekend, and where he and the others stayed out till eleven last year winning *Ghostbusters* mirrors and KISS bandannas and Mötley Crüe pins from the squirt-the-bull's-eye game, which was an utter cinch.

Two days later he is standing at the mirror again, this time pressing his finger to his cheek to remove an eyelash, a strange black fly-bristle, of a thing when his mom's voice goes hydroplaning up-up-up to say, "*Kev*-in, they're *he*-ere," and he grabs his jacket and speeds outside. A white Fiero is idling in the driveway, and Bateman's mom is at the wheel. She is allergic to gold, Bateman once told him—it turns her skin green. The car is a two-seater, so small that he has no choice but to buckle himself onto Bateman's lap, which jogs around beneath him as they gun off toward Roosevelt and the fairgrounds. "Ow, man, you're nothing but bone," Bateman complains.

"Shut up, man. You're nothing but fat. Hey, those can be our nicknames: Nothing Butt-Bone and Nothing Butt-Fat."

The silliness of the idea or the rat-a-tat of the words or maybe even just the two *butt*s—one butt is funny, two butts hilarious—Kevin doesn't know why, but the joke seems to work. Bateman catches himself laughing, then realizes how idiotic the line was and laughs even harder. Kevin knows the feeling. Occasionally, once or twice a month, the absurdity of a bad joke will make him laugh until he forgets to breathe, until the laughter itself becomes a kind of breathing, stretching back through time to fill his life, and he is convinced that it will never stop. The same thing happens with crying sometimes.

Between gasps Bateman shouts, "Mom, stoplight! Mom! Mom! Speed bump!" and in her cigarette-voice his mom says, "If you take them fast enough, you don't even notice they're there," and Kevin rocks back and forth with every turn in the road, every pothole, like the spring-headed cat on the dashboard.

Thad and Kenneth are already waiting inside the gate for them, hands stamped and tickets purchased, fixed to the pavement in their high-tops. "Where have you effers been?" they say, and, "We got here twenty gee dee emms ago."

It is a game of first letters.

"Yeah, dudes, sorry," Bateman says. "My mom took forever getting ready."

"In the bathroom? Taking a pee?"

"Nah, on the phone."

"*On* the pee."

"On the pee talking some ess."

"Just essing around with some jaying tee dee."

"*What*? What the fuck does that mean?"

"I have absolutely no idea."

Everyone but Kevin wants to ride the Zipper straightaway—he would rather stay right side up, thank you very much; he's declaring this an official no-barfing day—but he doesn't mind standing in line with the others. They inch along until they reach the rail where the operator is tearing tickets, and then Kevin steps aside to watch the small metal cages slant into the air and spin on their axes. It is an oddly sunless fall afternoon. The sky is the color of oatmeal with lots of milk. For a while he tries to zero in on Thad's blond hair, on Bateman's green shirt, but loop-de-looping his eyes around makes him dizzy, and eventually he just lets his gaze drift down the midway, listening for the great swooping arm of the ride to creak to a stop.

When his friends climb back out, Shane Wesson is with them. It is as if the Zipper has somehow given birth to him. Watching him stride over the asphalt, his cheeks red from the wind, Kevin has the impression that the ride has shaken something loose from him, and from Kenneth and Bateman and Thad and all the others, the thirty or forty people following the rail to the exit, so that whatever it is that usually keeps their minds hidden from view is gone, and every thought they have seems to pop right out of their faces. *Holy hell, that was fast. I should have worn the sweater instead of the windbreaker. Never, ever, ever, ever, ever, ever again.* He wants to turn to the person next to him and say, "Look, do you see that?" but he doesn't. The sensation vanishes as quickly as it arises.

He supposes he should still be angry with Shane, but the foxtail trick feels like a lifetime ago, and the truth is he has flat stopped caring.

All at once, Kenneth laughs and says, "I think some kid started *crying* on there," and Shane says, "Hey, Kev man, where'd you come from?" and Kevin says, "I don't know about you all, but I'm saving my emm for the gee."

"Say huh?"

"The Gravitron. My money for the Gravitron."

"Uh-huh." Shane drops a look. "So are you like *high* now, or are you like *black*?"

There is a mechanism inside Kevin that fixes an answer to every question, even the rhetorical ones. It moves forward a notch. "Whatever's awesomest," he says.

Now there are five of them, and they set off through the prize booths and the concession stands, past the barns that smell of sweat and hair and grass and corn and leather and milk and manure, past the thrill rides with their waves of colored lightbulbs. Music thumps up through their legs, a new song every thirty yards or so, booming out of the Himalaya and the Fireball, the Twister and the Screamin' Swing. Some of the rides turn in simple circles. Some rise straight into the air and plummet straight back to the ground, like a hammer centering on a nail. And others are less like rides than science experiments, Spirographing people through a complicated trajectory of loops and curves and rings-in-rings that Kevin could never reproduce on paper, not with a million tries. There is a game that involves dropping five metal disks into the outline of a circle that none of them can figure out how to win. There is a vendor wearing faded blue overalls who is selling fresh fruit and fried pickles. Kevin spends a good chunk of his allowance on a foam lizard attached to a long leash of coat-hanger wire, which scurries around like a live pet even if it does cost him four dollars. Four dollars, he thinks. That equals five comic books with three cents left over. Four dollars, which equals something like eleven candy bars. So much money. And he is so sure he will mislay the lizard in the tide of the crowd that eventually he does.

"How you doing with Mr. Lizard over there?" Bateman asks him, and Thad tries out a half-formed joke, "Mr. Lizard's World," and that's when Kevin realizes it is gone.

"I lost it." His eyes are as hot as coals. "Damn it, I lost it. Stupid fucking unbelievable shit. I cannot fucking believe this."

Kenneth corrects him: "It's right there in your hand, Kevin. Jesus."

And he's right—it is.

And the UFO whirs past overhead.

And the riders scream their midair screams.

And later he is inside the Gravitron, pinned to the cushion by centrifugal force, his scalp tingling under his hair, his feet floating up from the footrests, as the wall spins faster and faster. He can see himself in the mirrored column at the center of the platform, his jacket batwinged open beneath his arms. Beside him, a woman in a Panama Jack shirt tied in a high knot to display her stomach hollers along with the music. He looks on, first in the mirror and then in real life, as the tassel from her pants slides past her navel like a raindrop rolling up a windshield. She has the fallen-into-bed posture of a model in a perfume ad. It seems barely possible—a magnificent contest between gravity and centrifugal force—that the tassel will stretch far enough to slip beneath her shirt and touch her breast. Somewhere in back of the mirror, Sarah Bell is watching him tilt his head so that he won't get caught staring. She can tell what he is thinking. Anyone could.

After the ride, Thad distorts his face, making Pringles lips, and in his Goon voice, all strange and pipey, says, "I want to eat a fried pickle." The Goon voice is a total mystery. Kevin has always assumed that it is somehow connected to the Goon from Popeye, that great bald brute with the banana-squash nose, though how or why is hard to fathom. One thing: using the voice allows Thad to turn any remark, no matter how ordinary or sincere, into a joke. "I'm pretty sure that disk game is rigged, y'all." "My dad said he was gonna kick me in the crack of the ass." "I'm gonna do it, I'm gonna ask Annalise out. *No, Thad. But we can still be friends, Thad. Go away,*

Thad. Go away and leave me alone." The voice is his super-power. It reminds Kevin of Shadowcat, his favorite X-Man after Wolverine, whose intangibility lets her phase through walls and force fields.

Shane says, "Who would want to fry a pickle in the first place?"

"Whoever, I want to shake that man's hand."

"I want to shake his pickle."

"I want to pickle his shake."

"I want to fry his hand."

"Oh my God, did you just go, 'I want to *fry* his *hand*'?" Kenneth says, and it is two points to Kevin for the winning line.

Everyone else is sidetracked by the funnel cakes and corn dogs, but Kevin and Thad continue on to the fried pickle stand. Sometimes Kevin has no idea why he says the things he does. Why, for instance, as the two of them eat pickles from a paper plate behind the trailer, where a giant fan thickens the air with the smell of cooking oil, does he nudge Thad with his elbow as if he were passing him a note in class and go, "Hey, if the others start telling lies about us, like you were putting me down or I was putting you, we won't believe them, will we?"

In his Goon voice Thad answers, "What did that kid want with you anyway?"

"Kid?"

"When the rest of us were on that bus-looking thing that flipped over in midair, and you said if you rode it again you'd throw up—you know, that *kid*."

"Him."

The ride was called the Kamikaze. Kevin had been lying

next to it in the gravel when a boy's face had appeared above him like a pale moon.

"He just wanted to know if I was all right. I told him my head was spinning but yeah. He called me mister."

Thad strips the batter off a pickle with his teeth. "Wouldn't it be badass if we could float alongside the rides and pretend nothing special was happening? Like if we were just sitting there all la-di-da with our legs crossed, swooping around and around. People would fucking *freak*." His Adam's apple bobs in his throat. "These pickles, by the way? Totally disgusting."

It is an interesting expression, *la-di-da*. Kevin repeats it a few times. *La-di-da. La-di-da.* The wind gusts between the trailers, and a cotton candy cone goes somersaulting over the black extension cords, and from the far back of nowhere a memory comes to him, a few seconds of radiant filmstrip in which he is standing over a busy street, his eyes locked on a sunlit concrete ledge where an orange peel rocks back and forth like a baby's cradle. How old was he? he wonders. Where did it happen, and when? Was he alone? No, no, wait, he was holding the tail of someone's shirt, wasn't he? That shirt, he thinks—it is like a gap in a puzzle. If only he could remember whose it was, his life would fit together without a single missing piece. Would snap flat and turn into a picture. Would look the way it does on the box. For the rest of the day, he feels as if he is on the verge of understanding something momentous, something he knew long ago, knew to his bones and then forgot, a hundred years before he was alive.

The morning after the fair, he wakes on a pallet of blankets on Bateman's floor. The birds are calling to each other in twos and threes, and he lies there listening to them, testing himself for the sense of enlightenment he felt, or nearly felt, behind the food stand. It is somewhere nearby, burning its slow way toward him. And the next day, and the next, whenever he stops watching TV or reading comics for a while, letting his mind go clear and quiet, he can feel it fluttering inside him, thinning away little by little.

It is another two weeks before it vanishes completely. And what has he lost? Maybe nothing. He no longer knows. By then it is Halloween, and he is walking through CAC in a blond wig and a gingham dress, wearing a bra stuffed with balled-up hand towels.

He is one of eighty or ninety kids in costume. He catches a junior named Wesley Walls saying, "The few, the proud, the umpteen," and stores the line away to use with his friends, none of whom are there to hear it. Instead, crowded into the foyer and the gymnasium, are airline pilots and Draculas and three older girls dressed identically as flappers. There is a big gray battering ram of an eighth-grader in a lab coat and corpse makeup. There is a Cyndi Lauper and a Madonna and a Judd Nelson or a Judd Hirsch (Kevin can never remember which is which: the one from *The Breakfast Club*). And there are the usual cheerleaders and football players and drill team girls, costumed lazily as themselves. But no one else is gathering the same looks he is. He notices people turning as he passes—teachers, seniors even—their attention breathing lightly all over him. The tickling sensation he feels could be pleasure or it could be embarrassment. It's hard to tell.

Craig Bell corners him outside Bible and asks, "Exactly who are you supposed to be?"

He adjusts his cowboy hat. "Dolly Parton."

"Kevin . . ." Chris completes the thought by motioning up from the ground. "No. Just—*no*. You're not hairy enough to pretend you're a girl."

"What's that supposed to mean?"

"Put it like this: you look too much like a girl when you pretend you're a girl. It's disturbing. It weirds people out."

Kevin thinks of several comebacks, but he isn't happy with any of them. In the end he resorts to, "No, I don't. No, it isn't."

Though probably he is wrong. Probably he does, and it is, and good, and so what?

In the bathroom, before second period, when he takes his stance at one of the urinals and lifts the hem of his dress, the three older guys lined up beside him vanish into the hall like bottle rockets flying through a PVC pipe. As Kevin tucks himself into his underwear, someone else opens the door and does an instinctive about-face. *Whoosh*. It is like a game. At the mirror he adjusts his bra strap, dropping his shoulder and tugging at the elastic. Margaret Casciano watches him pick a flake of lipstick from his lips. She is one of those girls he has known since he was six, like Julia Harris and Tara Watson, so long that the thought of her should stir a thousand competing memories, but for some reason his mind always fetches up the same one: how in the fourth grade she sat behind him during a slideshow and in the dark, without speaking, scratched his back through his shirt.

Miss Vincent has already covered half the board with a pronoun chart. On the other half she is copying out a dozen numbered sentences. A cirrus cloud of chalk decorates her sleeve, raining traces of powder onto the floor. Kevin picks the smell up in his sinuses, that bitter scent of aspirin crushed with the back of a spoon. He takes his seat by the wall of comics she has clipped from the Sunday papers. So far, he has given her two strips to add to the collection, a *Marvin* with Bitsy the dog and a *B.C.* with Grog and the clams. She took both of them with an odd stretched smile he couldn't quite figure out. There was some strange brain work behind it—a reluctance, an embarrassment, *something*—she was trying hard to disguise as kindness. And there was also the actual kindness, the kindness that lay in the effort to wear a disguise in the first place. *I'm uncomfortable right now, but I'll try to keep it hidden. You're monumentally weird, but I'll stay quiet about it if you will.*

Pronouns are easy: he, she, me, you, nobody. Kevin listens with only half an ear as she conducts the lesson. He has a trick he likes to do with his pencil, angling the cylinder just so on the edge of his textbook, then watching as its tilt carries it up the desk. When he gets it exactly right, it will roll to the top of the book, fall off, and slide away toward the arm of his chair, tick-tacking over the polished wood like a log tumbling down a slope. It's the kind of thing he can do again and again, like playing catch with himself against his bedroom wall. He doesn't stop until Miss Vincent passes out the day's worksheet, which, as usual, he finishes before anyone else. "You know," she says to Kevin when he hands it in, "you're all the talk in the front office."

"*I* am?"

"You. They had a meeting to decide what to do about your costume."

"It's for Halloween."

"I know. That's what they decided."

"Decided what?"

"That you can cross-dress on Halloween."

"Yeah, and ultimately it was pretty easy. Mom had the dress left over from some square-dancing thing she did with her sorority."

In chapel, before the opening hymn, the air rings with footsteps and conversations, with six big sets of wooden bleachers cracking their joints. The sounds echo against the roof of the gym, coming back fuller and crisper. Kevin looks up, tracing the V-shaped struts and parallel lines of the metal girders. He has seen kids smack them with their palms after shimmying up the ropes in PE. From down here it seems nearly impossible. His own arms are like ribbons, and inevitably, when it's his turn, he just clings to the rope shaking until one of the coaches gives him permission to let go and leap to the mat. But what if he could crawl directly into the beams—there, from the side wall, where they almost touch the bleachers? And what if he was on the basketball team, and it was the final round of the playoffs against Oak Grove or PA, and CAC was behind by a single point, and at the last second he caught a wild throw from Steve Mollette, took aim at the basket from directly overhead, and *swish*: two points!—or would it be three?

He could be a champion, a star.

If only someone were watching.

Joseph Rimmer spots Kevin in his Dolly Parton getup and nudges Shane Roper, who says, "Man oh man! Thad told me you were all fagged up today, but I had no idea."

To which Kevin has no answer. He tries, "The few, the

proud, the umpteen," and Shane says, "*Umpteen?* Pray tell me, good sir, who is this *umpteen* of which you speak?" and Joseph says, "Umpteen Dumpteen sat on a wall," and they both break up laughing.

"It's like a bunch, isn't it? 'Umpteen'?" This from Sean Lanham, whose small round skull has inspired Coach Dale to name him Peahead. Nearly half the football team has been rechristened by the coach. Joseph Luigs is Moose; Barry Robertson, Curly; Randy Garrett, Hitman; Peter Vickerel, Pickle. With his thin arms and wheaty mustache, Coach looks too slight to be an athlete, but his voice seems to rumble up from somewhere far belowground, and the uncommonness of it, the surprising density, makes the nicknames he concocts sound affectionate rather than insulting. Let's face it: nicknames are cool. Kevin has always wished someone would give him one. But his real name, his full name, suits him too well already. *Why hello there, Kevin Brockmeier. Oh my God, did you see what Kevin Brockmeier's wearing? Mrs. Dial, Kevin Brockmeier keeps kicking the back of my chair.* He has never been—wait a minute. All fagged up?

Mr. Garland taps for quiet on the microphone, and Kevin finds himself wondering—did he understand Shane correctly? Did Thad call him a faggot? He remembers a conversation the two of them had once about the Bible, when Thad said, "It seems unfair that God would make someone gay and then send him to Hell for it," and before Kevin could answer added, "Shut up. I'm not a fag. Shut up."

It takes Thad two full periods to notice that Kevin isn't speaking to him. Today Kevin is the guy in the dress—that's what he's doing. He could suffer an epileptic seizure in total invisibility. *Look at those boobs heaving around on the floor. Look at that wig jerking back and forth.* Midway through lunch, Thad unwraps a giant Tootsie Roll, sets it on the bench behind Annalise, and points it out to the table. In his Goon voice he says, "Chocolatey chew."

Kevin gives a flat "Ha ha ha," and Thad makes a face. "What's got you so pissed off?"

"Oh, I don't know. Maybe something about you telling Shane I'm gay?"

"What? What the frick are you talking about?"

"I'm talking about me being quote-unquote 'all fagged up.'"

Honestly? Kevin appreciates the chance to act indignant. Sometimes jokes float into a conversation like soap bubbles—there they are, and you have to pop them. It's irresistible. He understands that. Kevin is wearing a dress, so he's gay—voilà!—joke accomplished. But if he gets angry, or if he has the right to be, then Thad will have to apologize, and what's the difference, really, between someone asking for forgiveness and someone asking for friendship?

"Just a minute now," Thad hedges. "Don't you remember at the fair, when you said we wouldn't believe anyone who lied about us?"

"So Shane's lying—is that what you're saying?"

"I'm saying we made a promise and—wait, you know what? Fuck off."

"Me fuck off?"

"Yeah, you, Islands-in-the-Stream." Clearly he has been holding the name in reserve. "Fuck off. You don't want to believe me, don't believe me."

"Fine. I don't want to believe you."

"Fine."

Outside, by the bluff above the field house, Shane Wesson is practicing his pitching, using clots of dirt he has pried from the bare ground at the treeline. He twists around on himself, then whips forward, over and over again, as if his bones are made of braided metal rope. One by one the balls disintegrate in midair, pattering down on the slope of brush and leaves. Kevin walks to the edge of the hill. There is a fringe of unmown grass beneath the rim. It nods in the wind, flexing up over the school lawn with the sound of someone dusting flour from his palms.

Kevin inserts himself in the sea of blue sky Shane is using for a strike zone. This time he knows exactly what will happen: the confrontation, and the shove, and that remarkable watched feeling of falling. The long rest of the day and the long rest of his life.

"Hey, man, what are you doing?" Shane says. "Get out of the way already," and Kevin faces him and says, "But I'm enjoying the view. It's such a beautiful day. Why should I go anywhere?"

Then the big hands are on his chest, and his dress blossoms up around his waist, and the weeds pour over him in a rush.

A dragon and a unicorn are playing tag, galloping past a man in a tunic and a demon with scaly green skin. *Myth Directions*, the book is called, and according to the list in front, it is the third volume in a series, after book one, *Another Fine Myth*, and book two, *Myth Conceptions*. Kevin found it in the checkout aisle at the grocery store, racked with the horrors and romances, all those fat glossy paperbacks in their tilting columns of black and cream. From the illustration alone—the flabbergasted expression on the man's face, the towelliness of the demon's bathrobe, the way the dragon was thrusting his tongue out—he knew he would love it, and he was right. It is amazing, enthralling, mythterious, mythchievous, unmythable.

At home now, lying on the floor with his head propped against his bedframe, which draws a hard indentation along the back of his skull, he interrupts his reading again to glance at the book's cover. He keeps waiting for the story to correspond to the picture. The dragon is named Gleep, the man Skeeve, the demon Aahz. So far there is no sign of the unicorn. Every chapter begins with a made-up quote, like " 'That's funny, I never have any trouble with service when I'm shopping.' —K. Kong" or " 'This contest has to be the dumbest thing I've ever seen.' —H. Cosell." It is totally hilarious—or supposed to be, anyway—and even when it isn't, it is at least

54

agreeable: funny in a jokey-uncle sort of way. It makes Kevin feel clever for getting what the *K* stands for, and the *H*. Ever since junior high began, several times and for no reason at all, he has woken in the small hours of the morning with the conviction that he's far from home and that his room, his posters, his comics, his record player—that none of it belongs to him. His desk is like an ancient altar on some faraway hilltop, standing beneath the ruined white moonscape of his ceiling. Where could he be? How did he get there? But he is never more comfortable, more at peace, than when he's stretched out on his carpet in the quiet of the afternoon, reading by the light of the window, the sun making the pages of his book glow like milk in a clear glass. He feels as if he was born here, right here, between his bed and his dresser. As if he has never moved so much as an inch.

After church on Sunday, he finishes the *Myth* book and puts it in his satchel with his worksheets, folders, and notebooks. He has never lost that old elementary school show-and-tell impulse, the sense that every cool new thing he discovers immediately becomes a part of him, a hallmark of his personality, with its own little interior ribbon-cutting ceremony. He has to carry it around with him, whatever it might be, or how will anyone know who he is?

In Bible the next day, before the bell rings, he shows the book to Ethan Carpenter. "This," he says, "is the single best thing I've ever read. I'm talking, *in my life*."

"Sweet. Can I borrow it?"

"What? No."

Mr. Garland has stepped across the hall to talk to Mr. Shoaf, and Leigh Cushman—a guy with a girl's name—is pacing at the chalkboard, smacking his palm with the back of his hand

55

like a substitute. "You kids're in big trouble. Take your seats. Stop talking right now, or you're all going to D-Hall. I mean it! This instant! That's it, every one of you's going to D-Hall. I'm giving you all checks. One check. Two checks. Corn Chex. Wheat Chex," and maybe in the end it was just a reflex, Kevin thinks, but if he had to guess, he would say that the reason he doesn't want to loan the book out, to Ethan or anyone else, is because of the part of his personality that is one gigantic record-keeping system, a complex sifting and filing scheme that dictates what goes here and what goes there, turning his life into so many marks on a tablet. His mind would busy itself with the book's whereabouts every second it was away. He knows it would.

"Okay, yes, you can borrow it, but Ethan? Look. You have to be careful."

"Dude . . ." Ethan says, meaning, *You've seen my comic books, haven't you?* His collection is as big as Kevin's—bigger even. He keeps it in a row of long white boxes he tends like a garden, gently maneuvering each issue into a clear Mylar bag with an acid-free board, then taping it shut, vertically not horizontally, so that the tape doesn't fray or separate, and arranging it with the others in alphabetical and numerical order. Side by side his comic boxes have the quality of giant Japanese fans, their slats closed *chock-chock-chock*. Kevin wouldn't be surprised to find out that Ethan dusts them.

He surrenders the book across the aisle as Mr. McCallum begins the morning announcements. Just like that it vanishes into Ethan's backpack, throwing a few scattered dots of color through the mesh of the front pocket.

For the rest of the day, Kevin feels the way he did that time he locked himself out of the house and saw his house key resting on the kitchen counter. The book is behind a window. The book is his, but he cannot touch it. Part of him would rather bike back to Kroger and buy another copy than wait for Ethan to return it. He is *Like That*, always *Like That*. He is no good at hiding it. A few Saturdays ago, sitting by the fountain at the JCPenney end of the shopping mall, he realized he was missing the bag with his butter mints and his pop-its and his *Song Hits Magazine*, and Kenneth said, "Kevin. Stop it. Good Lord. Look," gesturing to the ledge where he had set the bag while he was tying his shoes. "You're about to cry, aren't you? Why are you *like that* all the time?"

In SRA, Mrs. Bissard—Mrs. Bizarre, everyone calls her: it is irresistible—gives them a reading comprehension test, and as soon as Kevin has finished, he begins working on a detective story, the kind he has been writing ever since the first grade, hypothesizing that someone he knows, usually a kid from his class, has vanished, and he has been appointed to solve the crime. The Case of the Missing Sarah Watts. The Case of the Missing Craig Bateman. Or this time, for a change, a teacher: The Case of the Missing Miss Vincent.

He plunges into the mystery with, "The authorities were baffled," then sketches the facts of the case—how two days before, in fifth period, Miss Vincent had discovered Clint Fulkerson snoring at his desk and, when she couldn't wake him, left to fetch the principal.

"Aaaaaahhh! It was a scream, and, no doubt about it, it was Miss Vincent. The scream brought the whole school running. Clint had even awoken. When we got to the stairs, though, all we found were some ink stains. Miss Vincent had been teacher-napped!"

It's always the same for Kevin, the story gusting along

before him with its sails stretched tight, a boat seized by some strange and incredible wind. He relaxes his hold on it for PE, but only reluctantly. The whole time he and Alex Braswell are heaving the big leather boulder of the medicine ball back and forth, its casing scuffed and velveted like a walnut's, he continues to unravel the mystery's details. That evening, at home, he returns to his notebook. He assembles a list of suspects from the five students who were away from class when the abduction took place: Tommy Anderson, Chris Pickens, Scott Freeman, Sheila Watts, and Annalise Blair. Each of them, it turns out, was given a hall pass for exactly the same reason: to dispose of a leaky pen. *Aha! Ink! Like the ink in the stairwell!* he thinks. He deduces that Clint Fulkerson must have been drugged with sleeping powder, but when he investigates the filing cabinet in the office for evidence, he uncovers only "some confiscated candy, gum to be precise, and a paddle with a peculiar stain on it." The case seems hopeless. Then, suddenly, the criminal delivers a note to Kevin's locker:

> If you want to find Miss Vincent
> Then I'll give you just one clue
> The letter of where she is at
> Has the same letter as you!

You, he thinks. *U! The U Hobby Shop!* And sure enough, that's where he finds her, bound to a post in the basement. She tells him she was struck from behind, spilling her can of Diet Coke as she fell unconscious. It happened so fast that she cannot identify her assailant—but Kevin can.

The next morning, in chapel, he claims the microphone

from Coach McAteer and explains everything: how Clint was disabled with tranquilizers to drive Miss Vincent from the classroom, how the pens were sabotaged and the stair-well doctored with ink as a ruse, but how the criminal for-got one crucial piece of evidence: the paddle with its brown splashes of Diet Coke. And whose trademark drink is Diet Coke? Miss Vincent's. And who uses a paddle? The principal: Mr. McCallum! His villainy is inarguable, and he knows it. In desperation he brandishes a gun, but Kevin disarms him with a karate chop. "The police took Mr. McCallum to jail," he concludes. "I had succeeded and somehow knew this was only the beginning of my career as a detective."

There is a sound to finishing a story like the first note of the 3:30 bell. Inside him a great crowd goes pouring into the daylight.

The next morning, after Bible, Ethan returns Kevin's book, which he has read overnight in a single tremendous chug. He might be the single most efficient person Kevin knows—studying efficiently and falling asleep efficiently, spending his allowance efficiently and borrowing books effi-ciently. It is one of the five adjectives Kevin would use to describe him to a stranger: Ethan Carpenter is (1) efficient, (2) focused, (3) sarcastic, (4) truthful, and (5) amused. If he were a superhero, he would be Iron Man—or, in the DC Uni-verse, Green Lantern, the real one, Hal Jordan. "This book is awesome," he says. "When you're right, you're right. Just one problem, though: Where's the unicorn?"

"That's what *I* thought," Kevin says.

"I mean, he's right smack on the cover."

"I know."

"We should sue for false advertising."

"On principle *alone* we should sue."

"It would be like leaving Jesus out of the Bible—or not Jesus but, you know, Paul. Elijah. Who would be the unicorn in the Bible?"

"Shem."

Kevin often has to walk clear across CAC between classes. Because there is always the danger of a tardy slip, he carries half a day's books at once, trading the first set for the second immediately after geography. He tilts his way down the hall, pausing every so often to engineer the weight of his camera bag from one shoulder onto the other. Then he propels himself forward again. The bag is like a sack of cement, so heavy that its strap creaks to the rhythm of his footsteps. He sees older kids, and lots of them, strolling along with only a single book in their hands. They veer casually off toward their lockers as if school is just some temporary mix-up they've decided to tolerate for a while. They must exist in a totally different sort of time. Kevin wonders if they notice him at all, the skinny seventh-grader in the striped shirt slicing past them outside the lunchroom, counting his books to make sure he hasn't forgotten any.

Today, in English, they finish talking about subjects and begin talking about verbs. There are two kinds, Miss Vincent says, *linking* and *action*, and she gives them a handout with instructions to underline each verb and label it with either an *L* or an *A*. The worksheets are fresh from the ditto machine, and the paper bites at the air with its chemicals, each purple letter shedding a narrow outline of ink. Kevin ticks through the sentences one by one, then hands the assignment in along with the story he wrote. He is nervous—he can't help it. He feels the way he used to feel passing love notes to girls in elementary school. *Do you like me?* the notes always read. *Check yes or no.* But he is older now and his question is older, too, not *Do you like me?* but *Shouldn't someone?*

Check yes.

Check yes.

Check yes.

He pretends to study for science. Secretly, though, he watches Miss Vincent's expression as she flips through the pages of the story, the way her lips tighten at one corner but not the other, a smile with a limp to it.

What does it mean?

After the bell, she summons him to her desk and asks, "Is this for me to keep?"

"Well, no. But I can copy it out for you. Do you like it?"

"Kevin, it's great. So fun, and inventive, and cunning. It's like I'm watching a play, with actors and everything. I'm serious. You could stage this, and it would get a standing ovation."

"What about the Diet Coke part? Did you like that?"

"That part especially."

The usual slowpokes are jamming the stairs. It is against the rules to slide down the banister.

And all those love notes, he thinks. Dozens of them, one after another, daring somebody to say yes. In the fifth grade, in a fever of recklessness, he wrote to a different girl every few weeks, folding each letter into its own small packet, not one of those masterly arrangements with the pouches and the criss-crossing corners but the basic clumsy square that boys always made, delivering it to the cabinet where the kids filed their school supplies. *Do you like me? Do you?* Now and then he wanted a day where the something that happened was him. He remembers the exhilaration he felt waiting for the gossip to spread. In February, just before Valentine's Day, when everyone was always going with everyone else, he decided to make a play for Tara Watson. He biked with Bateman to the Balloonacy in Colony West and used his Christmas money to buy the store's largest balloon, a two-and-a-half-foot-wide Mylar heart, arranging to have it delivered to her at school. But the secret was too momentous for Bateman to keep. On Valentine's Day, by the time the knock came at the door midway through the afternoon, the whole class knew what to expect. They leaned forward to watch Miss Judy, the school secretary, steering the balloon sideways with her palm, guiding it awkwardly through the door like a zookeeper trying to coax an elephant into a cage, and a big thundering laugh ripped through the seats. Tara hid behind her lank blond hair, then fled the room crying. For the rest of the day, the valentine swayed in the currents above her desk, turning slowly on its crimped pink ribbon to display one side and then the other: the bright red face, the swollen silver mirror. Miss Taylor told Kevin that he was incorrigible. She had him look the word up in the dictionary.

Nearly two years have gone by since then. Now Tara is just another girl towering over him in the hallways. He can barely remember what it felt like to believe he was in love with her.

It doesn't matter.

The Case of the Missing Miss Vincent: A Play in Five Acts. It takes Kevin the rest of the day, but he is able to complete the script just before bed, rounding it off with a full list of the characters. He brushes his teeth, and he does his math home-work, and he slides the *Myth* book onto his bookcase, where it fills the gap it left as neatly as a rock prised from the clay. Then he turns out the lights and waits to forget himself, and after a while he must because it is morning.

Everything else seems to happen very quickly. By lunch Miss Vincent has read the play. He is cutting past the break room toward the Coke machines when she pulls him aside to suggest that he try mounting a production with some of the other seventh-graders, and that afternoon he gets an appointment with Coach McAteer, who agrees to assign him a date on the chapel schedule, "Let's see, why don't we say—oh—Thursday two weeks," and then Kevin rewrites the script in his most legible handwriting and asks his mom to Xerox the pages and holds auditions to select the actors, and Julia Harris is Miss Vincent, and Asa Stephens is Mr. McCallum, and Sean Hammons is Kevin Brockmeier, and Kevin himself is the narrator, and they meet in the library every day to rehearse their lines, along with the rest of the cast, the bit players, and no one wants to memorize the dialogue, it's way too much work, so fine, he says, whatever, they can carry their stupid scripts, and one day between classes he spies Annalise Blair saying, "Who me?," giving a palms-up gesture of amia-ble confusion, which is exactly how Anna Succhi, who depicts Annalise in the play, reacts when she learns she's a suspect in Miss Vincent's disappearance, and he wonders if there is a word for the kind of fame that makes it difficult to tell whether people are making fun of you, and two weeks have passed in a moment, and the show is premiering tomorrow, and he is carpooling home with Kenneth and Clay and Bateman, and the river is dotted with a thousand white circles, like confetti from a three-hole puncher, and Kevin prays for some force to whisk him a few miles further through his life and deposit him a day or two away, in that patch of sunlight blazing just up ahead, when the hard part will be over and he will not need to worry. But it doesn't work. It never does.

The next morning, at school, it can't be two minutes before Sean Hammons grabs him by the arm and pins him with a look of apology. "Kevin," he rasps, and *Bullshit*, Kevin thinks. *You're faking.* "I can't talk, man. I'm sorry. I've got laryngitis."

"Look—" Kevin begins. "C'mon—" But he can tell that Sean has settled on his decision. It's right there in his gaze, fixed in bold embarrassment.

All around them is the ratcheting noise of locker handles, the lapping and boiling of conversations, and Kevin's mind keeps offering up the same thought, over and over again, in the brightest of colors. "You're the star of the play. What am I supposed to do?"

Sean is all shoulders. "I'm sorry. I can't talk. I'm serious."

"So who's going to be me then?"

"You can."

"But I'm the narrator."

"Be both."

But the narrator is supposed to stand at one end of the stage, and Sean is supposed to follow the action: Kevin Brockmeier, the shrewd and fearless detective, dashing here and there after each new piece of evidence. That's how they've rehearsed it. Kevin can't be everywhere at once.

The first bell rings.

He has five minutes, he realizes, no more than that, to

hunt for a new lead actor. But his best friends are total chickens. Thad says he has stage fright, and so does Ethan, and Kenneth is in the other Bible class, and Bateman guffaws—*guffaw*-guffaws—and says, "No way. Nuh-uh. Find someone else to humiliate."

Finally Kevin manages to coax a yes out of Shane Wesson. Shane! He won't do any acting, he says, but he is willing to read the part of the narrator. "Take it or leave it, Kev."

"Thanks. You saved my life. So you'll meet us onstage?"

"Roger Wilco."

"Good. Over and out."

All right then: Shane Wesson will be the narrator, and Kevin Brockmeier will be Kevin Brockmeier, and Sean Hammons will have laryngitis.

After the second bell, Mr. Garland lowers the lights to use the overhead projector. In the humming gray dusk of the classroom, with the windows framing the cars and bushes, Kevin scans his script for what must be the thousandth time. He tries to concentrate on his new lines, but by now he knows the words so well that it's like reciting the Lord's Prayer or the Pledge of Allegiance. The meaning is buried far beneath the rhythm. *Our Father, who art the flag, hallowed by thy name.* How strange everything seems—Mike Beaumont doodling in the margins of his notebook, Saul Strong cleaning his fingernails, Matthew Connerly levering the back legs of Jim Boothby's desk up off the floor and then letting them crash back down.

"Boothby! Is there some problem you'd like to share with us?"

"No, sir. Sorry," and a second later, in a pissed-off whisper, "Quit it, Matt."

There they are, a roomful of people spending an ordinary hour at school while Kevin sits in the first seat of the third row, quietly burning to cinders. Go. *Go.* The clouds draw their shadows across the parking lot. The intercom scratches out an accidental rustle. He pays just enough attention to Mr. Garland to answer a question or two, but at the first clap of the chapel bell he launches himself into the hallway. He beats the crowd to the side door of the gym, drags the prop desks, microphone, and filing cabinet out from the wings of the stage, then waits in back for the rest of the cast to arrive, plucking at the odd machinery of ropes on the wall, arranged like the strings of a piano. One, two, Brandon Ostermueller. Four, five, Jennifer Graham. Ten plus himself, and that makes eleven. His cast. Beyond the curtain he spies a fragment of the basketball court, a thin band of yellow wall where faces appear and vanish atop long shimmers of clothing, but except for Ann Harold, who veers into the girls' locker room, he doesn't see anyone he knows.

The gym becomes saturated with voices. Then Coach McAteer silences everyone for the prayer and the opening hymn, the Mustang motto and the announcements. "Today," he says, "we have something special for you, a play presented by CAC's seventh-grade class, titled *The Case of the Missing Miss Vincent.*"

Kevin gives the signal to Joseph Luigs, Policeman #2, who is on curtain duty. He had imagined that taking the stage would be like diving into the ocean, but it is exactly the opposite, as if the dazzling lights have lifted him from the water and set him down on dry land. Life is so much easier without the salt spray and the buffeting of the waves. How come he never realized?

His nerves fall away from him in an instant as he projects his lines into the stillness. Acting isn't like he thought it would be. He is not a detective solving a crime, just himself, but a different version of himself, a better one, with an audience. From every side he hears the dialogue he wrote, all those jokes and hunches, screams and snores, *who-me*'s and sighs of relief, each of them coming at precisely the right moment. Shane has trouble deciphering Kevin's penmanship and keeps supplementing his lines with the stage directions: "It was two days ago and Miss Vincent was in her fifth-period class. Miss V. hits Clint over head three times with paddle—lightly but make it look hard." But otherwise the play ticks along without a blunder. All the bleacher sounds register in the darkness, every beeping watch and every popping joint. There are more laugh lines than Kevin realized, and when, at the climax, he karate chops the gun from Mr. McCallum's hand, the hoots of applause cause his heart to pound. He could be a movie star, a comedian, Howie Mandel, Ralph Macchio, Harrison Ford, anyone, anyone at all.

As soon as Miss Vincent has been rescued and the principal is safely in handcuffs, Kevin reveals the final piece of the mystery: "Clint Fulkerson had overheard Mr. McCallum talking to himself about the plan," he explains, "and Mr. McCallum caught him. So, at lunch, he sleeping-powdered Clint's drink so he wouldn't expose him."

That's it, his last line, and he feels as if the stage is spinning on a turntable, the way his bed seemed to do whenever he wore himself out as a kid.

Shane takes over again as the narrator: "Police walk out with Mr. McCallum. The police took Mr. McCallum to jail. I had succeeded and somehow knew this was only the beginning of my career as a detective." He dabs a "The End" lightly onto the end of the sentence, like calamine lotion.

It takes the audience a moment to realize the play is over. Once they do, they erupt in cheers. And okay, Kevin's not stupid, probably the applause is so loud because the performance ran longer than a sermon would, chopping a good fifteen minutes out of second period, but that's all right, he doesn't mind. You don't clap because you're overjoyed. You clap because it's time to clap.

The rest of the day glides lightly over the treetops and to the ground. Kevin has a funny sensation of freedom and blamelessness, as if he is secretly at school on some dream of a Saturday, pretending along with everyone else that it's important to attend class and obey the bells. The bulletin boards, the polished floors, even the fluorescent lights make him curiously happy. The whole giant building could cascade down around him in a sheet of water. It would hardly seem any less real. He wonders if this is how the others feel all year long.

In English, Miss Vincent hams it up for the class, holding her wrist to her brow and calling Kevin "my rescuer." In geography, Coach Dale gives him one of his certificates with the drawing of the hand making the A-OK sign—Attaboys, he calls them, and "I'm awarding this particular Attaboy to Mr. Brockmeier for being our Playwriter of the Year." And that afternoon, in PE, before dressing out, when Kevin joins the rest of the kids by the thick purple-and-gold mat Velcroed to the wall beneath the scoreboard, Bateman makes a point of posing his head on his neck just so and presenting an enormous laugh, a big barking show-offy thing that goes on and on and on. Kevin can't quite tell: Is he laughing because he thinks Kevin embarrassed himself, really and truly, or because he decided he would laugh and by God he's going to laugh?

By the next morning, the school is mostly itself again, with only a trace of yesterday's weird agreeability. Even that disappears when Ethan shows Kevin the book he found: *Another Fine Myth*, with Skeeve the magician, Aahz the demon, Gleep the dragon, and the ivy-haired assassin Tananda, her short dress spray-painted onto her curves. The four of them march along a cobblestone path between hillsides studded with castles and houses and evergreens.

Kevin can't believe it. "Where did you unearth that?"

"Lucky find. The B. Dalton in Park Plaza. They had the other three, too. Tananda is *hot*, isn't she? Way hotter than I pictured her."

"Wait. There are *three* others?"

"Yeah, mine and yours and *Myth Conceptions*, plus a new one called *Hit or Myth*, with Skeeve and Gleep and that same absentee unicorn on the cover. Except I bought this one, and it was their only copy. I'm waiting for my dad to give me my allowance, then I'm going to snag the others."

The bell sounds, and a couple of latecomers slip into their desks. The door stutters closed on its hinged brass doorstop. As Mr. Garland takes roll, Ethan tucks the novel into his backpack, trading it for his notebook, which he opens to a new page and headlines with the date and the name of the class. That handwriting! So well scrubbed, so meticulous. One time, in sixth grade, Thad said that it reminded him of a penis. It was such a strange remark to make, and yet so unexplainably true, that Kevin has never forgotten it. He wonders if he can convince his mom to drive him to Park Plaza tonight. It's important, he'll say. Mom, I have something I need to do. It's important. It's really important, Mom. I have someplace I need to go. I cannot get there fast enough.

They are crossing the wooded side of the building, Thad and Kenneth and Kevin, carving their way down the narrow belt of grass-stitched dirt. To the left of them are the red bricks, to the right the bare brown trees. Before them is the path, running along the slenderest of threads before it empties into the yellowing schoolyard. There is no door for Kevin to step through, no clearing where he can turn around. There is only this roofless natural corridor he cuts shorter with every stride, a rift between the bricks and the trees where their voices turn sharp and echo.

Bateman was with them when it started, standing at the light box of the Coke machine, but he peeled away before they left the lunchroom.

Now it is just the three of them. No one else.

Thad. Kenneth. Kevin.

Except that Kevin is out in front, and Thad and Kenneth are baying along behind him. So Kevin, then Thad and Kenneth, and between them a terrible howling few steps of space, which keeps diminishing and expanding, so that he never knows how close their voices will be when they come, or if he will feel their breath whisking across the back of his neck.

"Hey, Kevin, is it snack time yet?"

"By now it must be snack time."

"Yeah, isn't it snack time, Kevin?"

"I don't know about you guys, but I think I'm ready for a snack."

"For snack time let's share some M&M's."

"M&M's make friends."

It's as if they are tied to him with elastic cords. Each time they start to fall behind, he accidentally yanks them closer.

Maybe, Kevin thinks, if he doesn't say anything, if he just carries on walking with his coat wrapped around his body, holding his face to the smoke-gray sky, they will wear themselves out, the day will take some unimaginable hairpin turn, and they will change back into his friends. Yesterday they were his friends.

"Let's get some M&M's at the gas station," Thad says. "The gas station is where I like to get my M&M's. Where do you get your M&M's, Kenneth?"

"Same as everyone. Duh. The gas station."

"Me, too. The Superstop."

"It's super! The Superstop is super!"

"Super-*buh*."

"Superb," Kenneth agrees. "The perfect place for chips and candy. Today, for snack time, I don't know about you guys, but I recommend we walk to the gas station."

"Hey, Kevin, have you ever made a super stop?"

"Will you be our pal—our supe—our *super* pal, Kevin?"

"Can we spend the night with you and eat Steak-umms for dinner?"

"Super Steak-umms."

"Steak-umms at dinner*time*! And before bed*time*, at our pre-bed*time* snack *time*, can we eat some Crystal Light powder with a spoon, Kevin?"

"We love Steak-umms and Crystal Light powder."

"And M&M's."

"Yeah, M&M's."

"What do you say, Kevin?"

"Kevin."

"Kevin."

"Hey, Kevin."

"Super Kevin."

They are conducting an experiment. How many times can they say his name before it will become meaningless, like the pulsing of crickets, an empty, ugly music? What are the softest tools they can use to hurt him? The food he likes. The words he uses. What else?

"Hey, Kevin, when we spend the night, should we go to the mall or to the zoo?"

"Will you buy us some M&M's at the mall?"

"Or the zoo."

"Yeah, or the zoo."

"Some M&M's and shoe stickers?"

"And then will you lose the comic books you bought and start crying?"

"Is the giraffe your favorite animal at the zoo, Kevin?"

"Yeah, what's your favorite animal at the zoo, Kevin?"

"The giraffe? Is the giraffe your favorite animal?"

"Everybody has a favorite animal."

"It's favorites time! Time for favorites!"

They have turned the corner. Before them stretches the real world, where kids stand on the patio of the school eating chips and sandwiches and the clouds cascade over the parking lot, their reflections floating along on a great curved river of windshields. He sees Chuck and Alex in their letter jackets, and some ninth-graders massed by the hallway's glass doors, and girls, too, at least a dozen girls, with their white Keds and purses, earrings and cosmetics mirrors, and the sight of all those people whose lives are theirs, completely theirs, their lives and not his, people who have spent the last few minutes mingling in front of the school with no one looking for ways to hurt them, makes him feel unusually bold.

So far the ordeal—and that's what it is: an ordeal—has been private, a secret. Kevin senses that if he can take the next moment in his hands and bend it with just the right demonstration of relaxed confidence, like a strongman flexing a metal pipe, Thad and Kenneth will slip back into the habit of liking him. They'll do it. They will. They won't think twice.

As disinterestedly as he can, then, he pivots around and tells them, "Cut it out, guys."

But he has miscalculated.

They transform the words into a chant: "Cut it out, cut it out, cut it out, cut it out, guys." They stalk him across the grass as they recite it—just Kenneth at first, but then, quickly, both of them together. BOOM boom-boom. BOOM boom-boom. BOOM boom-boom. Boom-boom-boom BOOM. How do they agree so easily on the melody, without even rehearsing? It is a marvel. Cut the record and ship it to the stores and it will sell a million copies, filling the Camelots and Sam Goodys of the world. You'll hear it playing long after the needle has lifted from the platter. It's your heart, that's why, and it won't stop beating the time. And when the record wins a Grammy, they'll accept the trophy with an air of dumfounded good fortune. Where did it come from, such a beautiful song? They honestly couldn't say. Call it a gift from God.

They are following Kevin along the rim of the bluff, and nearby someone is laughing about something, and Carina DeCiccio slings her heavy black hair out of her eyes, and he has always been so nice to her, he's such a sweetheart, such a cutie, and maybe everyone is watching him, or maybe no one is, but don't ask him, because damn it if he's going to look.

Then the three of them are in the parking lot, Thad and Kenneth and Kevin, clipping through the aisles of cars. Thad interrupts the chant with, "Hey, Kevin. Hey, guy. Will you be our pal?"

"Yeah, our favorite pal?"

"Hey, little pal. Hey, little buddy."

"Our favorite little super pal guy?"

"Do you think Dolly Parton is super?"

"Dolly Parton!" Kenneth can't believe he didn't think of it first. "That's good—Dolly Parton."

"Do you think boobs are super?"

"Yeah, Kevin, don't you wish you had big boobs?"

"Are big boobs your favorites?"

"Big protruding boobs, like Dolly Parton's?"

"Protrusions."

"Protrusions are super."

"Is that why you wore that dress on Halloween, Kevin?"

"What are your favorite protrusions?"

Kevin knows better than to answer, but "I mean it," he hears himself saying. "Cut it out," and the trigger proves irresistible. They forget about Dolly Parton and take up the chant again. CUT it-out. CUT it-out. CUT it-out. Cut-it-out GUYS.

HERE he-is. AT the-school. WITH his-friends. Pun-ish-ing HIM. ALL he-wants. THEM to-tell. HIM is-why. What-did-he DO?

Thad tugs at the handle of a pickup, and it springs out of his fingers and chomps at the door. The sound is like a hole in the air.

"So, Kevin, could you fit your dick in this lock?"

"Hey, guy," Kenneth says to Thad, "cut it out."

"I'm sorry, guy."

"That's okay, guy."

"Don't mention it, guy."

Then Kenneth wonders, "Now which is it? I forget, so you'll have to remind me, Kevin. Is your dick *wide* enough but not *long* enough, or is it *long* enough but not *wide* enough?"

"My dick is my own business."

"Hey, hey, Jesus, Kevin. Whoa there. Why all the dick talk?"

"Yeah, guy. Why so much dick?"

"I think the guy has dick on the brain."

Once, in fourth grade, during recess, a bad kick of his sent the soccer ball leapfrogging over the yard into the street, where it burst beneath the tires of an eighteen-wheeler. A startling double explosion—*Bang! Bang!*—and then "Oh, *man*," the kids groaned, and "Great! *Now* what?" and Kevin crawled under a car in the visitors' lot. He lay there staring into the otherworld of springs and axles, thinking how funny it was of him, how clever, to persuade his classmates that he was hiding in embarrassment, when look at him, just look, resting happily on the cool asphalt, faking everyone out. He remembers it all so clearly.

The engine was painted with sprays of orange dirt. They looked like goldfish tails. The sun fell at a slant, making hunchbacks out of the shadows of the tires.

"I'm not paying any attention to you guy—to either one of you," he says.

"La la la" is Thad's answer, the tune of some daydreamy little kid tracing butterflies through a meadow. "La la la. La la la," and Kenneth follows along with him. "La la la la la."

Their tongues add a strange thrust to each syllable, as if something wholly beyond their control is happening. The sound is an egg, and they can't keep it from hatching.

"Is it snack time yet, Kevin? You still haven't told us if it's snack time."

"Yeah, can you point us to the nearest Superstop?"

"La la la."

"La la la la."

"La Kevin la snack la la."

"La Steak-umms la la."

"Hey, Kevin, are you still going with that hot girl from Eight Wheels?"

"Yeah, is that hot girl still your girlfriend? Why haven't you introduced us to her yet?"

Hard to believe he has heard the same voices coming from two ragged old sleeping bags on the floor of his bedroom— Kenneth and Thad, the best of his best friends, mimicking Coach Dale, or warbling that Freddie Krueger song, or arguing over pinup girls: Heather Locklear or Heather Thomas?

Kenneth says Kevin's name again, and Thad asks him what's wrong, is something wrong, pal, he sure hopes nothing is wrong. They pursue him past the cars at the end of the lot, and then over the crooked line of pavement that vanishes into the dirt, and then around back of the building, where the PE class has been playing horseshoes in the afternoon, flinging U's of steel at the two notched stakes of rebar in the soil. If they reach the first stake, Kevin says to himself, he will stop walking. He will face them and demand they leave him alone, because it's not going to work, Thad, he won't let you bait him, Kenneth, he's one hundred percent totally fucking serious.

His voice will not break. He will keep himself from flinching.

Okay, if they reach the second.

"You didn't answer us, Kevin. What's wrong?"

" 'Cause we're only trying to help. How can we help if you won't talk to us?"

"I have an idea. Why don't we share some M&M's?"

"M&M's make friends."

Kevin whirls around and says, "Why are you doing this? Leave me alone. I'm dead serious."

Kenneth makes scare-hands. "Deadly!" he says. "I'm deadly! Total deadliness!"

Thad starts blinking with a queer sunburnt expression. It looks as if he's waking from a poolside nap, becoming aware little by little of the sting in his senses. Kenneth says, "Perfect. That's perfect," and duplicates the expression.

There they are, their eyes glimmering with imaginary tears, their mouths open just wide enough to show that their teeth don't meet, and the awkwardness, the fretfulness, the amazement in their faces—Kevin realizes that it is their imitation of him. They must have practiced it, and carefully, when he wasn't around.

This is the big premiere: Kevin About to Cry. Lights. Music. Curtains.

"Is it crying time?" Thad says.

"It's time to cry," Kenneth says. "Time to cry, guy."

"Go the fuck to hell," Kevin says. "I mean it."

Then the bell for fifth period rings, and they shadow him inside, repeating, "Go the fuck to hell, go the fuck to hell, go the fuck to hell," the most hilarious joke they have ever heard in a long lifetime of hilarious jokes.

He can't believe he still has half a day of school to survive—math and SRA, then PE and the locker room, then the slow parade of parents in their vans and Broncos and station wagons, with Thad and Kenneth waiting beside him on the sidewalk for their rides. For all he knows, they might decide to start the whole routine over again. Kevin's mind won't stop replaying the details. *Snack time gas station Crystal Light Dolly Parton la la la Eight Wheels is something wrong, guy?* Worse, he keeps confronting the sight of himself on their faces. He's not vain or conceited or anything. It's not like he stands at the mirror every day brimming with tears to examine what it does to his reflection. And the truth is that unless you count that age-old photo of him on the toddler train at the amusement park, sobbing in his white shirt and red denims, today marks the first time he has seen how he looks teetering on the verge of crying. So *that's* him, he thinks—a little kid blinking at the unfairness of it all.

Lately he has been seeing the kind of person he is more and more clearly. He could never be anyone but himself. Who would have guessed, though, how much of himself he did not yet know?

IN-the-halls. EV-ery-one. SEEMS-to-be. Staring-at-HIM.

ALL-right-boys. TIME-to-start. BOM-bard-ment. Go-get-dressed-OUT.

SOME-thing-wrong. MIS-ter-B? DO-you-need—? No-Coach-I'm-FINE.

And the most humiliating thing of all is how long the two of them must have been storing up their material. Kevin imagines a thousand conversations about him, stretching back through Thanksgiving and Halloween, homecoming and Mazzio's, the countless arcade trips and sleepovers of the summer, back as far as Mississippi, as far as sixth grade. He can practically hear their voices: *Have you seen the way negro looks when he's trying not to cry? I know, and he has to have a favorite everything. A favorite state capital. A favorite monster. "It's gotta be the werewolf." The werewolf! "Oh, yeah, it's gotta be the werewolf." And Holy Christ, what's with that "la la la" crap?*

That night, in bed, though he stays as quiet as he can, he can't help producing a funny faint animal noise, like the rickety breaths the footballers make in the weight room, which is okay, he supposes, as long as his mom doesn't hear him. Finally, some membrane or fiber in his throat seems to snap like a piece of chalk and he falls silent. He didn't realize his body could make such a sound. What the hell was it?

The next morning Kenneth's mom is on carpool duty. Kevin can't explain why, but something about the way Kenneth slouches in the passenger seat, fast-forwarding through the sucky songs on a Night Ranger tape, makes Kevin guess that the lesson, or experiment, or punishment, or initiation—he doesn't know what to call it—the ordeal. He guesses that it's over. Bateman says something about Mrs. Bissard, and Kevin makes the usual joke, "Mrs. Bizarre," and Kenneth cracks out a quick note of laughter.

And that's when Kevin is sure of it: it's finished, exhausted. He's officially out of danger.

At lunch, though, when he approaches their table, Kenneth and Thad begin their interrogation again—"What's up, guy?" "How ya doing, guy?"—and Oh God, he thinks, where is he supposed to sit?

They get up and follow him as he tries to leave. This time he stakes out a deserted patch of wall beside the lockers.

"So what about that girl from Eight Wheels, Kevin? You two still going together?"

"Damn, man, that chick was fine. What did you say her name was?"

"Yeah, Kevin, you told us her name, now didn't you? What was it again?"

"Cheryl?"

"Wanda?"

"Priscilla?"

The first two are obviously fictitious. The third is the name Thad uses for his fat-lady jokes.

"It's Sonya," Kevin tells them, and maybe it even sounds plausible, but in reality he made it up last year when he decided to trick everyone into believing he had a girlfriend. Sonya liked to call him every night at 8:45—8:45 on the dot. Sonya told him about all the films she recorded off HBO, Showtime, and the Movie Channel, mainly musicals—*Grease 2* and *Eddie and the Cruisers*, *Annie* and *The Best Little Whorehouse in Texas*, plus her favorite, *The Pirate Movie*. Sonya liked him because he was smart and funny. She was one of the older girls who had colonized the pinball machines at the skating rink, the same machines Kevin and the others adopted on dares to deliver battery-shocks to themselves, standing deep back between them and bridging the current with their fingers. She is real, but he has never actually spoken to her. "And like I said, we broke up."

"Oh, *tha-at's* right. You broke up."

"They broke up."

"Unfortunately," Kevin says, "yes. We broke up."

"So did you two ever make out?"

"Is she a tonguer? I bet she's a tonguer."

"Did she give you a hickey?"

"Did she rub you off?"

"Did you suck her protrusions?"

He doesn't understand it. He watched them so intently during chapel, roosting just a few feet away, and that's the most bewildering thing of all—how they could sit there praying and singing as if everything was normal and the middle of the day wasn't looming ahead of them like a giant stone wall. Even now they don't let any obvious cruelty show, only camaraderie, agreeability, the most genuine curiosity. What's wrong, Kevin? What? They're just flicking questions at him. They're barely touching him. This? It's just a chuck on the shoulder, pal. Don't mistake it for a punch.

The next day, Thad greets him in the hallway before science with, "*Buenos días*, Detective Kevin," and by lunch he and Kenneth have added the name to their volley of questions. Sometimes it is difficult to tell what is a taunt and what isn't. *Detective Kevin* counts but not *buenos días*, the gas station but not the mall, *guy* but not *man*, Steak-umms but not comic books—why?

"Buying some Fritos, Detective Kevin?"

"Fritos fan?"

"Hey, maybe we can eat some Fritos together the next time we spend the night with you."

"And you can show us your *TV Guide* collection."

"Yeah, *TV Guide*s kick major ass."

"So when can we spend the night with you again? Friday?"

"Or how about Saturday?"

"Hey, Detective Kevin," Kenneth says, "whatever happened to those chips you used to bring in the plain silver bags. You know the ones—"

"Mystery Chips," Thad answers.

"That's right! Mystery Chips! Perfect! A mystery! Detective Kevin is on the case."

The day after that, they move on to the girls in the class: "Man, Kevin, you won't believe this, but I heard that Annalise Blair really likes you."

"Yeah, I heard that Rachel Brierley likes you, too."

"Honor Shelton said that you were hot."

"Noelle Batch wants to have your babies. Twins, didn't she say, Kenneth?"

"Yep. Twins."

"Twins. Sonya and Priscilla."

Every room is like a math problem. Thad in one desk plus Kenneth in another equals Thad and Kenneth. Thad tapping the lid of a soda can plus Kenneth raking his hand through his hair equals Thad and Kenneth. Occasionally, if Kevin moves silently, unassumingly, and stays out of their line of vision—if he sits with Ethan, say, or Bateman—they will fail to notice him, or choose to ignore him if they do, but usually some muscular reflex seems to seize them as soon as he passes by, and with barely a pause, like ghosts in a video game, they are up and after him.

"Why, hey there, Kevin."

"Where you off to, Detective?"

"Feeling kind of la la la today?"

"What's up, Detective La?" and the name is so entertaining, so surprisingly fitting, that it takes over the conversation. "Oh, Detective La, that's great. That's the best one yet. So is it going to be M&M's or Fritos today, Detective La?"

"Sarah or Melissa, Detective La?"

"Hey, dude, give Detective La some room. He's got to weigh his options."

One afternoon Kevin blocks Thad's path through the lunchroom and asks, "What's this all about? Thad, tell me. You have to tell me. Why are you guys doing this?" but Thad keeps listing back and forth at the waist like someone struggling to stay upright, glancing at the wall or the mainstays, anywhere but at Kevin, and "No," he says. "I can't. Man, leave me alone," as if Kevin is cheating, and all his appeals, his sad grasps at the past—what is he thinking? He should know better. That shit isn't part of the game.

After school, Clay's mom collects the carpoolers in her station wagon. Kevin climbs over the rear seat onto the cargo shelf. As they pull away, he flashes his finger at Thad through the back window. "Whoa," Kenneth says, impressed. "He honestly looked shocked by that."

But by the next morning, the gesture is just another part of their routine, the two of them contorting their hands in outlandish palsies, holding their middle fingers as straight and as slender as candles on a cupcake. Apparently, when you flip someone off, you are supposed to use your index and ring fingers as a sort of pedestal, bending them both at the first knuckle. Kevin does it wrong. It makes him look queer.

At lunch, Thad and Kenneth find him drinking from the water fountain in the foyer and come lunging over with their fingers extended. "What does *this* mean? Hey, Kevin, what is *this* supposed to mean?"

Before he can stop himself, he has said it again, "Cut it out," and they have struck up the chant: "Cut it out. Cut it out. Cut it out. Cut it out, guys." This time Shane Wesson is with them.

They trail Kevin into one of the stairwells, calling him Kevin-guy and Detective La and asking, "What time is it? Do you know what time it is? Pardon me, but by any chance do you think you can tell me the time?" The stairs smell of Pine-Sol and shoe leather. Shane lifts him up off the floor and pins him against the wall, giving a bullish grunt of exertion. He means no harm, not really, or if he does, it's only because he always means a little harm, thinks it's funny to mean a little harm. He is taller and stronger than Kevin—considerably—but there is a guilelessness to the way he overpowers him, clashing up against him for the sake of the joke. He sees heaving Kevin into the wall as his role in the performance, just as Kenneth's and Thad's roles are to make crying faces, and Kevin's is to pretend he's being bullied. The situation demands it of them.

And the crazy part is that Kevin is often barely a hair away from imagining that Shane is right, as if, out of boredom or whimsy or some sharp new teenage impatience, Thad and Kenneth have made up their minds to put on a cloak of hostility, and he is playing along with them because they are his friends and it seems to make them happy. He could put a stop to it with a single word. He is ninety percent sure. But then the two of them will select some incident from a few weeks or months or even years ago, one he never would have guessed they remembered, much less found foolish or contemptible, and present it to him with all the edges sharpened. The hurt of it will hit him sudden and hard. His life will become real again. It always happens the same way. There are days when he is lucky enough to evade them, but not many.

One lunchtime midway through December, when the sky is spitting just enough rain to keep everyone inside, he spots them craning their necks for him in the hallway, and he retreats upstairs to the quiet row of classrooms where the senior high kids are working. It is Miss Vincent's free period, and she is eating a sandwich at her desk. He knocks on her open door and asks, "Do you mind if I hang out here until the bell rings?" She has just taken a bite, and she beckons him inside with a feint of her chin.

Kevin heads for his regular seat beneath the wall of comic strips, a paling rainbow of *Marvin*s and *Momma*s and *Hi and Lois*es, their corners creased over rectangles of Scotch tape.

Miss Vincent gives him a probing look and asks, "Kevin, is everything all right?"

The sound of his name. That's all it takes. From someone who doesn't mean it as an insult.

"Oh dear," Miss Vincent says, and "Take your time," and "Would you like me to close the door? Here, let me close the door."

Haltingly, because it is not a story, he tells her what has

happened. The rain taps like grains of rice against the glass. A laugh filters through the wall. When he has finished, Miss Vincent gets up and walks to her desk, tugs out a handful of Kleenex, and hands them to him in a lily. In elementary school, on the first day of class, everyone was required to contribute a box of Kleenex to the supply cabinet. They never lasted until Christmas.

"How long has all of this been going on?" Miss Vincent asks.

"Two weeks. More like three."

And that's when the intercom goes off, and the building fills with noise, and her tenth-graders begin to arrive. She escorts Kevin to the landing at the top of the back staircase. "I need you to wait here a few minutes. Can you do that? I'm going to page Mr. McCallum. He'll want to talk to you."

"But I've got math."

"Don't worry about math. I'll write you a pass."

"But—"

The fire door sighs closed on its metal cylinder. He sinks down the wall to the floor. There is no silence like a school's after the halls have drained and the bell has rung and the doors have clapped shut like a string of firecrackers. Kevin rubs his eyes. For a moment, his body seems to swim with light. He hears Miss Vincent call his name from the corridor, but he is sitting directly beneath the grated window, and she can't see him. "Kevin?" she repeats, and a wild guilt goes sprawling through him. He wishes that he understood where it came from. Often he has a dream—he could be inside it now—that he is carrying something fragile, something precious, and he has dropped it. Sometimes he relives the accident a hundred times before he wakes up. He can never prevent it. That's how he feels listening to Miss Vincent say, "I don't know what to tell you. He was right here. I don't know where he went"—as if something irreplaceable has bobbled from his fingers. It is falling, it is broken, and maybe it will always be broken. A week might pass, a year, and who can say?

. . . .

There is no silence like a school's after the halls have drained
and the bell has rung and the doors have clapped shut like
a string of firecrackers. Kevin rubs his eyes. For a moment,
his body seems to swim with light. By the time his vision has
cleared, a man is standing over him on the landing, a skinny
guy with the look of a guidance counselor on his day off,
untucked but still buttoned up. The man holds himself with
the same slight hunch Kevin wears when he wants to remain
invisible—except stiffer, old-mannier. Here, Kevin thinks, is
someone who has been trying to go unnoticed for so long that
the posture has become irremovable. He is welded into it.

Breathlessly, like a runner finishing a race, he says Kevin's name, giving a sympathetic dip of his chin. "Hello again.
You're supposed to follow me."

Without thinking, Kevin gets up and accompanies him
downstairs. They both skip the last step with an instinctive
little elastic stride, as if they're avoiding a puddle.

If you had asked him, Kevin would have said he was sure
the stairwell door opened at the back corner of the lunchroom, but the wall must have spun ten feet to the left, because
they end up in the kitchen instead, behind the Formica counter where the science club and the spirit squad conduct their
pizza sales. The man leads him through a darkened side room,

KEVIN BROCKMEIER

then past the vending machines and microwaves to the table where Asa Stephens and Danny Morgan usually sit.

He makes a jellyfish gesture with his fingers: *Have a seat.*

Kevin takes the bench across from him. He has never seen the lunchroom so deserted. He can hear the Coke machines humming like spaceships.

"So," the man says—a finished statement. "It's been pretty awful, hasn't it?"

"Thad and Kenneth and everything. Yeah. Am I supposed to go over it all again with you?"

"You can if you want."

"Well, I just finished telling Miss Vincent, and she said—" On the table Kevin notices a pattern of sunlight guttering through leaves. He turns to face the row of windows. "Hey, it stopped raining."

"For now it has, absolutely."

"Weird. Where's Mr. McCallum, anyway? Shouldn't he be here for this? Miss Vincent said she was going to call the principal."

"Mr. McCallum is waiting upstairs for you. I promise he'll stay there as long as it takes."

Kevin scrutinizes the man: his lean neck, his dark beard, the pigment spots on his forehead. His mannerisms are oddly familiar, like those of some halfway relative in the background of a hundred family photos, all mild words and big stage gestures. He has one prominent canine tooth. His eyeglasses are shaped like elongated stop signs. And the way his hair thins to silk on top and flares back in a great puff at the sides reminds Kevin of—oh—what was his name?—that small skullish guy who commanded the Death Star. "You're not a guidance counselor, are you," Kevin says.

"A guidance counselor, that's good!" The man has a generous laugh, much bigger than it appears he would. Each *ha* is like a perfect circle, soaring out of him one after the other, a tunnel of glowing blue rings. "A guidance counselor! No, think of me as a sort of chaperone. A courier."

"So you don't want to talk about Thad and Kenneth?"

"Well, again, we can if you'd like, but no. Truth is, I know the Thad and Kenneth story already. By heart. What I want is to offer you a way out."

"I'm sorry?"

"Here, look. This is—will turn out to have been—the worst few weeks of—well, your childhood, at least. Your school years. That I can promise you, Kevin. Right now you think the harm is irreparable, and you know what? You're right. It is irreparable. It is. You've changed. From now on, for good or ill, however fractionally, you're going to be a different person."

The transparent hairs on Kevin's arms prickle.

"I know, I know, you don't want to be a different person. Believe me, I understand. And that's why I'm here. Life is difficult and confusing, but—and here's the thing—it comes with an escape switch. Everyone gets their chance to press it if they want. This is yours."

He situates his glasses on his forehead. Some people's eyes seem to soften without their glasses. His, though, sharpen to a knife-edge. "Do you understand what I mean?"

"Not the remotest clue."

"No? Look around."

Kevin can't stop sniffling. He wipes his nose with one of the Kleenex Miss Vincent gave him. When he was a kid, in first and second grade, he would cry so furiously sometimes that his jaw ached and sweat pasted his hair to his scalp, yet ten minutes later he would feel fine, magnificent, as fresh as grass. But now that kind of crying leaves him utterly exhausted. For the rest of the day his eyes will have an ugly red-rimmed look, with colorless flats of tightened skin underneath. Between classes he will hog the water fountain, drinking until his stomach strains at his jeans, but his throat will keep itching anyway. He won't begin to feel better until he gets home and turns on the TV.

"The lunchroom," he says to the man. "Big whoop."

"Look closer."

At first there is just a vague weaving of colors that keeps flickering behind itself, returning and disappearing, but then some warp seems to move through the room, and it all settles into place. Everywhere Kevin turns, pairs of figures are joined in what must be conversation. Some of them look like people, a few like animals, a few more like animals if animals were people: two gangling birds with long snaky necks, two mice sitting back on their haunches, two coppery-red toad-things, rows of polished feelers along their backs that look like paper clips bent partway open. Many of the shapes are hardly like bodies at all, but gadgets, magic tricks, science experiments. Kevin isn't quite sure how he recognizes them as living creatures at all, only that he does.

Two spikes of beating light.

Two plumes of yellow-brown smoke that slip through some pinprick in the air.

Two curved sheets of paper marked with letters he can't read.

A pattern of frost slicing its way through a similar but sparser pattern.

Some strange roughening in space next to a slightly more porous roughening.

Two plantlike sprays of greenery twitching with raindrops from an approaching storm.

Two mirrors reflecting everything except each other.

Why, Kevin wonders, didn't he notice any of them earlier?

"Who are all these people?" he asks.

"They're like you. Alive. This is their chance to say no."

"But where did they come from?"

"Everywhere."

"But I mean what are they doing *here*?"

"Here at CAC? That's just a convenience, an illusion. Right now they're probably wondering what you're doing under the ocean or in the forest or between the solar rifts. Anyway, none of that matters. What matters is how you answer the question."

Kevin cocks his head to one side. *The question?*

"The question is, Would you like to press the escape switch?"

A hissing gradually takes the shape of the room, squaring out against the walls and the ceiling. It sounds as if a blank tape is playing directly into his ears. Usually Kevin feels smarter than this.

"I don't understand."

The man pivots his head until a vertebra in his neck pops. "Mmm. What I'm saying is that you're alive, but you don't have to be. You don't have *to have been*, ever. It's up to you. That's part of the bargain. This is your chance—your one chance—to make up your mind."

Two old women hobble through a door Kevin can't locate once it closes. The man points to the bench where they were sitting and says, "See, that was her chance, just now," then to a pair of threads winding around an invisible spool. "And this is his."

Something inside Kevin lands suddenly. He takes a sharp breath and tells the man he understands, but not out loud. What should he do? The man repositions his glasses. "I know nearly as much about you as you do, but I'm here only to ask the question. You'll have to answer it yourself."

"But we just met."

"Meaning how can I possibly know anything about you? Let's try this." He bows his head, and his scalp gleams through his hair. "Flash paper. Ice Pirates. Fool's gold. Magnets. World War Three. Orange peel. Incorrigible. 'It's casual.'" None of it would make sense to anyone but Kevin. "And do you remember that E.T. thing you used to do, the way you'd extend your neck and flex it until the joints cracked? And then one day you heard Stacey Leavitt say, 'He's doing it again,' and realized it was weird. Oh, and what about the dream you always have that you're at the flea market, and you're sorting through a box of comics, and you find those two issues of *Captain Carrot* you're missing. Or the time your dad called out of the blue, and you guessed it was him before you picked up the phone, and you answered with, 'Hi, Dad,' as if you were psychic. Remember? You were living at Sturbridge. Mom had just made dinner: spaghetti. And how about that bare patch in the yard at Clapboard Hill that looked like a giant's footprint? And that pencil collection you had in the second grade? And here's one: how about that same year, when Miss Jordan wouldn't lend you the bathroom pass and you decided you'd teach her a lesson by wetting your pants—"

"Okay. Stop."

"—and you sat on your math workbook—"

"Stop. I get it."

"—to soak up the puddle."

"Enough."

With his palms, the man surrenders. "And it's Grand Moff Tarkin. From *Star Wars*."

On the table alongside theirs Kevin sees two small girls with strands of glass melting from their fingernails. One table over are two amoebas of red oil paint, and by the wall are a heap of zigzags in several shades of gray, and near the break room are two men wearing suits of yellow tennis ball fuzz—or no, wait, that's their skin—and "What's going to happen when Miss Vincent comes downstairs looking for me?" Kevin asks. "Or when someone cuts through the lunchroom on their way to the office? Won't they freak?"

"No one's going to interrupt us."

"But what if they do?"

"They won't. But tell you what, why don't you go upstairs and check on them? You remember the door we came in by? Use that same one."

Kevin takes the stairs two at a time. The fire door at the top opens with a big *cha-kunk* of its push bar, and in seconds he is on the other side and gunning out into the hallway. He nearly runs into Miss Vincent and Mr. McCallum, who go as still as cats. They were on their way to find him, just as he knew they would be, their faces locked in expressions of worry and anger. He is about to apologize for leaving without permission when he notices how Mr. McCallum's legs are bent, how Miss Vincent's skirt is hanging at three different angles, none of them down, and realizes that they aren't moving. At all. They look like statues clothed in skin and hair and fabric and color and softness and light.

Gingerly he steps past them and peeks into English. Everyone is motionless. A John Paul Wornock statue is standing at Miss Vincent's desk, leaning his weight onto her stapler. A Cindy Jones statue is asking a Paige Adair statue a question. The window is spotted with raindrops. Behind them the sky is the meaty gray-brown of an oyster. Is it raining or is it not?

Down the hall Kevin steals a glance into Coach Strand's class, then into Mrs. Bissard's.

Statues.

So the odd balding man in the lunchroom was right: no one is going to interrupt them.

He can't resist a quick step outside. At the bottom of the stairs, before he approaches the extra door, the one opening into the kitchen, he tries another, the door leading to the wooded slope in back of the building. It takes him a moment to comprehend the view and to reassure himself that he recognizes it. The rocks, the trees, the bricks, the air conditioner—one by one he marks them present in the roll book. They are all exactly where they should be, fixed against the backdrop of the highway—yes—but not frozen like the people upstairs. Their shapes are cut through with movement, their colors filled with a simmering brilliance, as if every one of them is a world of small explosions. The sweet gum balls flicker like candles in metal cups. The pine needles glow like spray lamps. He watches a squirrel trip by in a cluster of sparks, the particles of its body throbbing and dancing, then plunge through the brush and into the forest. What would become of him if he followed it, he wonders, if he let the door shut behind him and strode out into the trees?

In the lunchroom the man is leaning over the table, rubbing his eyelids. Kevin sits down and asks him, "What exactly happens if I press the escape switch?"

"Your life will no longer have taken place."

"Yeah, but where would I *go*?"

"Where do you think you would go?"

"I think my friends would believe I had died. Wouldn't my friends believe I had died?"

"Your friends would have no idea who you were, because you would no longer have been born at all."

"I don't see how that's possible."

"Maybe not, but creatures are disappearing from existence as if they had never been all the time. The ones who die aren't the ones who disappeared. They're the ones who decided to stay."

To his left an elderly woman with hair dyed the color of an emery board strokes the lush red curls of a little girl. To his right two globes of what looks like Elmer's glue wobble across the floor on a cushion of static electricity.

"Look, think of the world as an ocean whose volume is constantly changing. Remove a drop of water or add one, it doesn't matter. The ocean will simply accommodate the difference. There's an effect, of course, but it's negligible. Now if a whale disappeared, it might change the fortune of its pod. If a ship disappeared, it might change the fortune of its fleet. But we're talking about the water itself, and the water is always flowing. You're a drop of water mistaking yourself for a whale."

"So do I know people who have pressed the escape switch?"

"You mean *you* you? No. But some other version of you, in a different world? Almost certainly. Except that that other version was transformed into this one when the people who would otherwise have shaped your life disappeared."

Kevin pictures himself with a tremendous gang of duplicates, hundreds and hundreds of them trailing away behind him, like the long tunnel of images he can control from his barber chair at Fantastic Sams, each earlobe, cheekbone, and shoulder a millimeter deeper inside mirrorworld. The sight of those thousand Kevins in their thousand black smocks has always been his favorite part of getting his hair cut.

"And what if I don't want to press the escape switch right now? Will I get another chance?"

"Well, no. That would make the whole dilemma meaningless, wouldn't it? Like wishing for more wishes."

"So this is it?"

"It. Absolutely."

"Then here's my question. Let's say my life keeps going. What will happen with Thad and Kenneth and me? Can we be friends again?"

"Hmm." The man is tugging at his beard, gathering it into a devil's point. "Here's what I know. Starting today, they'll leave you alone, or mostly they will—but no, Kevin, I'm sorry, you won't be friends again. The two of them will transfer to public school after eighth grade: Forest Heights and then Hall. You'll hardly see them again. One night, during your junior year, they'll turn into your driveway when they spot you hauling the trash to the curb—I don't know why. Some reflex. They'll sit there with the motor running, trading *hi*'s and *what's-going-on*'s with you, all of you old enough to drive, on the verge of vanishing into your adulthoods. By then they'll seem like emissaries from a different world. *Oh, that's right*, you'll think. *Thad and Kenneth. We were best friends once.*"

"You know all that?"

"I'm not as foolish as I look."

"What about girls? Girlfriends?"

"I'm not going to lie to you, that's going to take a while. I'm not sure I should tell you. You'll be just shy of thirty."

"Jesus!"

"I know, I know, I'm sorry."

There they go again, his glasses, over his eyebrows and onto his forehead.

"But then you don't really want a girlfriend, do you? What you want is to *wish* for a girlfriend—and you can do that *now*, by yourself, without relying on anyone at all. You want the little pulse of drama that comes from feeling you adore a girl, and that your life and hers might be transfigured at any second, and that the reason your Friday night at the football game or your Saturday afternoon at the movies isn't as wonderful as it could be is because there's someone out there who hasn't quite realized she loves you. The truth? I think you want to fantasize about girls without actually accommodating your life to one. You don't want to risk disappointing yourself by coaxing your way into some girl's affections and failing to love her. You don't want to *choose* somebody, because that will mean you can't choose somebody else. And the only way you can keep believing you're secretly irresistible and yet doomed to live without love is by never putting yourself to the test. It's a mess. A wilderness of contradictions. Every year it will leave you feeling uglier and uglier, more and more tired. You'll have to become much more limber if you intend to maneuver your way out of it."

Kevin draws his breath to speak, but doesn't say anything.

"Sarah Bell? No. In ninth grade, she'll sit directly in front of you in English. You'll prop your leg along the edge of her chair occasionally, letting your calf settle against her hip. It will feel like the absolute outer limit of your bravery. One day you'll place your hand on the shoulder of her chair, and she'll cross her own hand under her arm, where no one else can see it, and lay it on top of yours. The rest of your body will go completely lifeless, but your palm? Your fingers? Man! They'll flare with these ten thousand points of heat, as if all the nerve endings have turned to match heads. Neither of you will move—will so much as *twitch*—until the bell rings. The thing is, you'll never be able to decide if she was flirting with you or just screwing with you. You'll be twenty-eight and teaching creative writing at UALR when her cousin tells you she's gotten married."

"Wait. So I'm going to be a teacher?"

"No. Well—every so often. Mainly you're going to write books."

Books.

"Like the *Myth* series?" Kevin asks.

"What's that now? Oh! Those. I had forgotten about those." A slanted nod, and the man says, "Maybe a little like the *Myth* series. Not much."

"Will I do the covers, too?"

"Just the writing."

"So I'll be famous."

"Well, no, I wouldn't say so."

Kevin imagines himself filling sheet after sheet of notebook paper, in cursive, in some impossibly distant future, his hand traveling over the pages in jags and quivers, as swiftly as the needle of a lie detector, while he sits at the kind of desk that lawyers use, in a chair so plush and imposing he will feel like a preschooler nestled in someone's lap. The image is rich with detail, but when he tries to visualize his own face, he sees only a grown-up scramble of pores, stubble, and wrinkles, some white hair here and some pink lips there and two dark eyes shining like thumbtacks.

"How old will I be when I die?" he asks.

"How old will you be when you *die*. That I can't tell you."

"What else *can* you tell me?"

"Here, you want the rough outline? At fifteen, you'll leave CAC for an arts magnet—Parkview, down past the Target on John Barrow. You know the beginning of *Nova*, that shot where all the planets go spinning off into the distance? At first it will feel like that, as if the Earth is hurtling away from you, fast, but give it a report card or two, and Parkview will surprise you by becoming your life, and a better life than the one you've left behind. By the end of tenth grade, you'll lose touch with everyone you used to know at CAC, all of them but Ethan Carpenter. Oh, sure, you'll hear about people in bits and pieces—that Bateman has started a lawn service, that Alex is coaching basketball, that Margaret is working at a bank—but you won't be involved with them anymore except in memory, so the news won't be gossip to you, just journalism. In your twenties you'll see Chuck Carnahan at the airport and marvel at his Southern accent. Has his voice changed that much since junior high, or did you simply fail to notice the drawl he had back then because you had one, too? High school—that's when you'll make the friends you'll keep. Three perfect years of falls and winters and springs. It will feel as if the seasons are defining themselves once and for all. You'll envision yourself as a lawyer your sophomore year, an actor your junior year, a writer by the time you graduate. You'll play at being in love, and once or twice you'll wonder if you really are. You'll leave Little Rock for college and grad school, and then you'll return. You'll never drink. You'll never smoke. You'll write stories, and eventually they'll add up to books. You'll experience your twenties as a decade of timidity, doubt, suspension, and your thirties as a decade of illness. I suppose if you walk through life saying *no*, *no*, *no* often enough, it's only a matter of time before the world starts saying *no* back. Eventually, slowly, like someone picking his way out of a rockfall, you'll begin to feel better, though you'll never really trust the foundations of your life again, or believe that they're solid enough not to crumble. Sometimes you'll suspect that you made your home once and for all at age seventeen, and that everything that's happened since will always seem slightly alien to you, slightly contingent. Your instinct will tell you that answering machines truly exist, but not cell phones. Computers, but not the Internet. Your puberty, but not your hair loss. There was a time you understood, you'll think, and you're living in its aftermath, and even though you'll see the world's changes shimmering around you with their own reality, you can't help expecting that they'll all disappear one day and you'll wake up at home before you left. You built your stronghold years and years ago and sent yourself into adulthood as a kind of advance scout—that's how it will feel. And you'll keep thinking that someday soon, with the knowledge you've gathered, you'll go back in time and begin again. Surely it must be possible."

Behind him two bent old men, twins, sit mumbling in their suits and bow ties. The one in the hat gives a teacherly shake of his finger. The other laughs out loud, his front teeth picture-framed in gold.

"There's more," the man says, "but I'm afraid that's as far as I can take you."

"Wait. Okay. So now that I know all this stuff, won't everything be different? Can't I use what you've told me to change my future?"

"No. If you decide to return to the time stream, you won't remember any of this. It's the same for everybody. One opportunity to answer the question. Then you either resume your life, just as it was, or you extinguish it."

"So all of this—?"

"A scene on the cutting room floor."

"Who are you exactly?" Kevin asks. "Will I see you again?"

"No." The man squeezes his mouth shut, takes a shuddering breath, and sighs through his nostrils—his attempt at a polite yawn. "Or not like this at least. Forgive me. Long day. But yes, in a way, eventually you'll see me. Absolutely. So then." He digs his thumb into the cord of muscle at the side of his neck. "Have you made up your mind? Would you like to press the escape switch?"

Watching him, Kevin feels a tightness in his neck. He massages it with his fingers. He thinks about the awfulness of riding to school these last few mornings, the way his feet seem to pin him to the floorboards. He thinks about the rain honeycombing the screen of his bedroom window, the laundry basket giving off its smell of sweat and plastic, his cat's voice box motoring away on top of the VCR. He thinks about the Tupperware pitchers in the refrigerator—the orange one filled with Crystal Light, the yellow one with iced tea. He thinks about the racks of comics at Gadzooks. He thinks about Thad and Kenneth stalking him through the school, saying his name like a curse word, and about houseflies and candy bar wrappers and blades of grass, all of them filled with the boiling brightness of the sun. He has a test in PE this afternoon. The tapes he ordered from Columbia House must be in today's mail, and if not in today's then surely tomorrow's. He might turn out to love his life. Who can say?

"Send me back."

The man nods *all right*. He gestures for Kevin to follow him. Together they leave the lunchroom, walking past a young girl with an infant in her lap, then two carpet-like masses of swaying brown fiber, then two willowy figures with tunnels of empty space where their eyes should be, stray circles of wall and vending machine showing through them from behind.

On the landing at the top of the stairs, Kevin lowers himself to the floor. He waits to see what the man will do next. Again he feels as if he is getting his hair cut, but his least favorite part this time, bracing himself not to giggle as the trimmer buzzes up and down his neck. The man makes a motion so small it is barely a motion at all. For a moment the stairwell looks like a drawing of itself, the steps and the baseboard, the uprights and handrail changing into black lines on white paper. Kevin rubs his eyes. His body seems to swim with light. He hears Miss Vincent call his name from the corridor, but he is sitting directly beneath the grated window, and she can't see him. "Kevin?" she repeats, and a wild guilt goes sprawling through him. He wishes that he understood where it came from.

. . . .

The school is asleep in the drizzling rain. From Mr. Weatherly's room comes a burst of laughter like a balloon popping: pierce a crowd with a needle, and *bang!*—that's the noise it will make. It vanishes in an instant, the seconds sliding closed around it, so quickly that Kevin might almost believe it had never happened, except that the quiet in the hallway seems fuller, deeper, just the *tap-tap-tap* of dress shoes and the softer sound of Reeboks.

He is following Mr. McCallum to his office. Once or twice, glancing up, he sees the principal make a little sideways movement of his chin, as if to discourage a bug from touching down, but it is December and too cold for bugs. Kevin guesses he must be rehearsing his questions. *Now tell me, who started all this exactly? When did they begin, would you say, these difficulties of yours? I'm sorry to hear that, but whose fault do you think it was? Is that so? Is it? Then why did you wait so long to speak up? Can you look me in the eyes, right now, Mr. Brockmeier, and contend that you're one hundred percent certain you didn't get exactly what you deserve?*

Nothing in the world is one hundred percent certain.

Really? You and I are both here talking to each other—isn't that one hundred percent certain?

Maybe ninety-nine-dot-nine-nine-nine percent. Everything could all be a dream.

*So what you're saying is that the trouble you've been hav-
ing might in fact have been your fault? It's possible, you're
saying?*

Not at all. You're distorting my words.

And just like that Kevin is lost in a reverie of debate.

That's not what I meant, he says, and you know it.

Yes, technically, sure, anything is possible, he says, *but so
what?* Possible *isn't the same as* true.

Well, sir, he says, *if you're looking for absolute proof, I can't
give it to you. No one can. Prove one thing absolutely. Go
ahead. I'm waiting.*

But as soon as Mr. McCallum guides him to one of the
padded chairs by his desk and lowers his gaze to listen more
carefully, encouraging him to "Take your time now, son. Go
ahead. Talk to me," the argument in Kevin's head ceases, and
a surge of confession billows through him. He can't help it. A
Scout is trustworthy, loyal, helpful, friendly, courteous, kind,
obedient, cheerful, thrifty, brave, clean, and reverent. On my
honor, I will do my best to do my duty to God and my country, to obey the Scout law, to help other people at all times, to
keep myself physically strong, mentally awake, and morally
straight. Adults make Kevin uneasy. They always have, and
they always will. With teachers he knows how to be a good
student, with parents a good kid, but beyond those borders is
a no-man's-land of bullets and broken earth. The sight of it
stretching in at him from the distance, so gigantic and impen-
etrable, frightens the living hell out of him. He has never
been able to have a difficult conversation with a grown-up
without leaking nervous tears—tears of shock, not sadness or
pain—and this time is no different. The room seems to flicker
through a projector. He can feel his cheeks becoming wet. He

tries to restrict himself to a bare handful of important facts, the stairwell and the parking lot and *Cut it out, guys,* but each detail reminds him of another, a third and a fourth and a fifth, and with every tiny particular, his memories grow further out of their shape. The story is such a hard one to be his.

Mr. McCallum wants to know more about the time Shane Wesson heaved him against the wall, of all things. "Stop right there, Kevin. Did anyone else grab you, trip you, push you, or hit you? Physically, I'm talking. With their hands." He seizes the air like a pair of shoulders.

"No, just Shane."

But what, Kevin wonders, does *that* have to do with anything? Shane isn't the problem. Shane didn't hurt my feelings. Shane didn't even *mean* it.

"So no one else laid a hand on you?"

"I don't think so."

"It was Shane and Shane alone?"

"Yeah." Blink. "But he didn't bother me so much."

"All right. Continue."

"Thad and Kenneth were the actual instigators," he says, and the time has come to describe the *la la la*'s. It was their most perfectly engineered bit of teasing, he tells Mr. McCallum, perfect because it was so simple, just the two of them adding *la*'s to the conversation, one after another, like bricks, and Kevin trying to speak around the corners, until before long, in the quiet of his imagination, he began adding the word himself: *la la, la la, la la la.* They had done something to the word so that it was not itself anymore. He could hear it faintly behind everything he said, and sometimes he still can, and maybe he will forever. The bell sounds the same in the office as it does in class—not any softer and, surprisingly, not any louder. The noise of students fills the hall like a flock of birds shotgunning out of a tree. Though Mr. McCallum seems not to notice the commotion, Kevin has to stifle the urge to collect his books and take off at a stride. He will be the last person across the building: the loser.

"You know SRA's fixing to start. I'm about to miss roll."

"SRA . . . that's Mrs. Bissard, right? I'll give you a tardy pass. Mrs. Bissard will understand. Anyway, we're nearly done here, aren't we?"

Kevin's not so sure, but "I guess so," he says.

A few minutes later, when he leaves the office, Thad and Kenneth are already waiting in the outer room. They pretend not to notice him, unlike Shane, who arrives with his backpack slung from his shoulder, wearing the snow-day look of someone without a care in the world. He says, "Hey, what's up, K.B.? Where you been?" as he passes Kevin in the doorway. Then he frogs him cheerfully on the biceps. It is the usual harmless jab, the one all the guys trade with each other in the locker room, and if it bruises Kevin, that's only because he is puny.

That night, during Kevin's last few minutes of phone time, Bateman calls to tell him about the punishment the principal handed down: a week's detention for Thad and Kenneth and a two-day suspension for Shane. "Two-day vacation, more like," Bateman says. "Hell, two full fucking weeks."

Christmas begins on Friday—that's what he means. It will be 1986 by the time Shane returns to school. "So what will it take for you to get me suspended, too?" Bateman asks. "I figure (a) I can shove you against a wall, or (b) you can catch me drinking beer at school, or (c) doing drugs, or (d) I can stab you."

Bateman says: "I'm easy. Take your pick."

He says: "There's also electrocution."

He says: *I'm joking so the hard part is over.*

He says: *We're still friends, you and me.*

Percy is trotting across the kitchen toward his water dish, his tiny steps so exact and unvarying that Kevin always imagines the floor is simply sliding into place beneath his paws, like a giant moving sidewalk. The microwave shows 9:00 and then 9:01. From the VCR he hears the first tinkling music-box notes of *All My Children*. Before his mom can tell him it's getting pretty late, isn't it, my goodness, will you look at the time, he says to Bateman, "Hey, man, I gotta go. See you tomorrow," and Bateman says, "Okay. Stab you tomorrow," and Kevin returns the phone to its cradle.

He shakes a few chicken-flavored Bonkers into his palm. Percy changes course, snapping the treats up, then harvesting the spice from Kevin's fingers with his tongue. Kevin scratches his brow, that funny flat spot where it looks as if styling gel has been combed through his fur. He is a long silver muffler of an animal, so agreeable that sometimes Kevin walks around the house wearing him draped across the back of his neck, his little round head perking this way and that. Once, in the middle of the night, playing on top of the washer-dryer, Percy tipped the laundry basket down around himself, meowing from behind its bars until Kevin woke up and let him out. And last week, aiming for the Christmas tree topper, a kind of dunce cap with a big silver star, he landed a foot too low, clambering through the branches until the whole construction came crashing to the carpet in a hurricane of lights and tinsel. For once Kevin is going to keep him overnight. Jeff, home from school with a fever, has been monopolizing him all week. Does Percy get bored, Kevin wonders, watching him read a *West Coast Avengers* and change into his sweats? What would he say if he could speak? As usual, at bedtime, Kevin tries to get him to stay under the covers, but he would rather trot along the bedspread and bat at the lumps of Kevin's feet. Eventually, he cozies up against the backs of his knees. Kevin can feel his purr rumbling into him through the layers of sheets and blankets. Either that or he simply hears it so clearly he imagines he can feel it. The sound keeps softening and escalating with Percy's breathing, like a car navigating a switchback. The restfulness of it makes Kevin's mind hum. It is almost enough to make him believe he has never felt any other way.

The next day, before Bible, Thad crouches next to Kevin's desk and asks him if he still likes Billy Joel. He pronounces the name with the penned-up destructiveness of someone cracking an egg against a frying pan: Billy-Joel *tack-tack*.

Kevin can't believe it is starting again. "Billy Joel's a hell of a lot better than Mötley Crüe," he says, and braces himself for the repercussions, but Thad just stares at him and "Jeez," he says, "I was only wondering. Bite a guy's head off, why don't you."

Boothby, Braswell, Brockmeier, Brooks: Thad's seat is right behind Kevin's. He takes it without another word, and why not? The way he holds Kevin's gaze says everything. Kevin likes Billy Joel. No one but gaybaits likes Billy Joel. Figure it out.

Maybe—probably—the only reason Thad stays so quiet is because he doesn't want to get in trouble, but that's okay with Kevin. He'll take circumspection over open abuse any day.

Following English, just as the bell is releasing everyone to third period, Miss Vincent gives him a greeting card with a drawing of a hippo standing on its hind legs. She hands it across his desk unassumingly, offhandedly, like homework, and no one pays much attention. Though the caption looks handwritten, it isn't: "When everything really starts to get to you, DON'T DESPAIR! DON'T GIVE UP! Just do what I do," and on the inside, "Eat." There beneath the punch line is the blue ink of her cursive, full of circles, like the pattern at the corners of a fancy napkin: "Hope you are feeling better about things today. Things will get better, just be patient. Have a good day! Love— Ms. Vincent."

The words make a kind of drumbeat in Kevin's head.

Things, things. Better, better. Love.

Things, things. Better, better. Love.

For nearly an hour he listens to it, opening the card every so often to read the note again, and then geography has ended, and he is surveying the lunchroom. Where should he sit? The Thad table is an impossibility, and so are the girl tables. And the majority of the others are already taken by older students, eighth- and ninth-graders who have known each other for most of a lifetime.

Kevin shoulders up against one of the pillars. Too many people aren't his friends. He feels as if the sheen of paint on the walls, the fluorescent lamp sputtering above the door, the shadows of the tree branches on the windows are all whispering a secret to him, one he could hear if the rest of the kids would just be quiet, something about time and school and where his life is taking him, but instead there is only the popcorn of everyone's voices, bursting and bursting and bursting.

He decides to sit with Leigh Cushman and Mike Beaumont. He finds a barnacle of gum on the underside of the table and picks at it with his fingernails. Before long Saul Strong joins them with his sandwich bag and his Ruffles and "Hey there," he greets them. "It's the Tough Guys," which is the name they have given their volleyball team in PE. They've even invented a chant:

We're tough guys! We don't take no crap
When we deliver our TOUGH RAP!

"How's it going with y'all?"

"*How's it going?*" Leigh complains. "I'm totally gonna fail this Bible test, that's how. Are you gonna fail it? 'Cause I am. All those begats and he-dieds and crap."

"See, you just don't remember memory verses. That's *your* problem."

"My point exactly! I only remember things I already know. That's what they should have: *knowing* verses."

"' 'Cause knowing is half the battle,' " Mike says.

"Meep meep," Kevin adds.

Saul shakes his head. His feathered hair does a little landslide. "Man, that's the Road Runner, not G.I. Joe."

"No, no, there's this episode where Shipwreck kicks a coyote into a canyon, and when it lands, he says meep meep. It's a Road Runner *joke*, not a Road Runner *mistake*."

"My whole *life* is a Road Runner joke," Leigh says.

"*My* whole life is a Road Runner mistake," Kevin says.

He's not sure what he means, or if he even means anything at all, but the tone of sad-sack defeat in his voice gets him a laugh.

The result is incontestable. That's who he is: funny.

The rest of the day passes somehow, and then he is lying on his bedroom floor staring at the blades of the ceiling fan, edged with ruffs of gray dust, and there is only Friday to finish before Christmas break.

He spends most of the evening working on the lyrics of a Christmas song—"Deck the School," he calls it—the kind of parody he has written by the dozens ever since he started buying *Mad*s and *Cracked*s from the magazine rack at Kroger. The verses ascend through the school grades, each one landing squarely on a big-name student, a Beau Dawkins or a Bryan Plumlee, a Matthew Connerly or a Doug Odom. The next morning Kevin deposits the page anonymously on Mr. Garland's desk and waits for him to read it. You never know with Mr. Garland. You just never do. He is half jester and half grouch. Telling a joke in his class is as likely to earn you a demerit as a laugh. But after the bell rings and the quiz begins, when he finally lays his fingers on the page, he chuckles silently with his mouth closed, exercising one side of his face as if he is working the sugar off a jawbreaker.

In chapel, sitting with the rest of the seventh-graders at the far end of the bleachers, Kevin watches him take the microphone and announce, "The kid who wrote this actually included all the fa-la-las, but I'm just going to give you the good stuff." Mr. Garland delivers the lines like wisecracks, pausing to let the laughter burn down to ashes. The loudest reaction comes from the eighth-graders, for "When we get back, there'll be no lickin's / Assuming that there's no Chris Pickens," and then from the seniors, for "Can you hear the women screamin'? / There's mistletoe and (gasp!) Scott Freeman."

Afterward, in the thick of the applause, a voice shouts out, "Who wrote it?" and Mr. Garland tacks the paper to the stand with his finger. "Sorry, folks. 'By anonymous.'"

Someone once told Kevin that if a hummingbird's wings stop, its heart will explode.

That afternoon, following seventh period, Ethan Carpenter invites him to a Friday-night movie with his youth group. Kevin calls his mom from the pay phone in the foyer to ask permission.

"To spend the night, you mean?"

"*Can* I?"

"Yes. I suppose. If it's all right with Ethan's parents. Have them call me."

There is no better place to sleep than away from home. He and Ethan wait at the loop for Ethan's dad, watching the cars vibrate slowly down the carpool lane, Kevin tolling the big metal school bell gently with one of his knuckles. They go shuddering through town in the old Chevy van Ethan's dad uses to deliver cigarette cartons. The carpets are saturated with the mushroom-and-cinnamon smell of tobacco, and Craig O'Neill is DJing on KKYK, and Ethan can't get used to Spider-Man's new black costume. "I don't know. Call me a sucker for tradition. Spider-Man isn't supposed to be the Punisher." His dad leaves them at the foot of Ethan's driveway, pulling away with a cheep of his horn. Other people's houses are always too bright or too dark. Ethan's is somehow both, with its small square cave of a living room and its bedroom glazed white with sunshine. "I'm hungry," he says. "You hungry? Let's see what we got here." They eat pudding pops out of the freezer, and corn dogs out of the microwave, and then Ethan's mom drops them off at the big brown moon-dome of the Cinema 150, with its giant screen curving across the auditorium like a tipped-over rainbow. Sarah Bell sits one row behind them, between Jess and another girl. Every so often Sarah's clothing will rustle as she recrosses her legs, Sarah's knee will jog the back of his chair, Sarah's stomach will produce a bearlike rumble, and Jess will say, "Hungry much?" The movie is about Sherlock Holmes as a high school student, and Kevin and Ethan both agree: take away the gargoyles and the stained-glass knight, and what's left? It's no *Raiders*, no *Jedi*. It can go away. Goodbye.

"So we've got this party at the youth minister's house," Ethan says. "We can catch a ride out there with someone, or I can call my folks to pick us up. What do you think?"

"Who all's gonna be there?"

"Pretty much everyone you see."

Which means Jess and Margaret and Tara and Kristen and Julia, all the Pleasant Valley Church of Christers.

"Everyone?"

Ethan has the face of someone wresting his tongue around for a sesame seed. A "yes" filters out of him like a sigh. "Yes. Sarah's going to be there."

They take a bench in one of the church vans. Their breath is whitening the air, and their hands are jammed in their pockets, and the heater begins to blow, and the tires whisper over the asphalt, and a half-moon hangs low in the sky, and the traffic exhaust makes the stoplights look like open paint cans, round glosses of color with little coils of light inside, and it is not so hard to believe that anything can happen on a cold night, at the beginning of Christmas, with girls. They roll up University, past House of Hobbies and Discount Records and TCBY, and "I've gotta tell you," Kevin says, "I'm kind of surprised the church would take you guys to a PG-13 movie."

"Wait, that was PG, wasn't it?" Ethan says.

"PG-13," one of the older kids says, "for violence."

"And pipe-smoking," someone adds.

"And lameness."

"Anyway," says Ethan, "there aren't any rules against that sort of thing. We're all thirteen."

"*You're* not."

"In two weeks! Give me a break!"

Kevin's family used to be Catholic, but now they are Methodist. He has never attended any church other than St. James—not since he was a little kid—but going to chapel at CAC has taught him that the Church of Christ is against all the same things his is, plus a few random extras: organ music, dancing, co-ed swimming. Back in October, during a sermon, Superintendent Diles outraged some of the kids when he divided the school's Church of Christers and its non–Church of Christgoers into two separate categories, "the Christians here and all the rest of you."

"I'm as Christian as anyone else," Kevin remembers hearing afterward, and "It's like he's saying we're not going to Heaven," and maybe some people were angry only because they believed they *should* be angry, they had a responsibility, but others seemed truly indignant.

That same afternoon, waiting in the bleachers for PE to

start, Kevin said to Ethan, "You don't really think that, do you? That all Methodists are going to Hell?"

Saying the word—*all* those Bible words: *hell, damn, Jesus*—felt like cussing.

"Nah. The way I look at it is that how God wants you to live is like a point at the center of a circle. You should try to figure out where that point is and live as close to it as possible, but God wants us all in Heaven with Him, and salvation's a pretty big circle."

"*You're* a pretty big circle."

It was the obvious joke, and Ethan knuckle-punched him on the shoulder.

"Ow. See, it's funny 'cause it makes no sense."

The punch didn't leave a bruise, just a tiny constellation of scarlet dots that were there when he went to bed but gone by the time he woke up. For the next few days Kevin couldn't stop thinking about Ethan's invisible moving circle of sin and forgiveness. He felt as if God was tracing him everywhere he went, sliding His eyes this way and that as he walked to the Superstop or kicked the soccer ball against his fence, ran laps around the school gym or collected his lunch from his locker. And still, occasionally, Kevin imagines he is drifting around inside the big glass ring of God's grace. With every lie, every favor, every compliment, every dirty joke, every act of meanness or goodness, selfishness or decency, he goes bobbing around before God's eyes like an animal plunging through the crosshairs of a gun. Someday God will fire, and Kevin will die. If God hits him, he will go to Heaven. If God misses, he will go to Hell.

The van carries them past Grady's Pizza and the Mole Hole, then past the barbecue joint where the grill smoke flows from an old black cannon in the parking lot, and then under a bridge where a deserted basketball court lies spread out in the lamplight like a scene at the bottom of a pool, a dozen layers of algae straining the sun to a thin green gloss. Little Rock keeps taking him by surprise. Shopping malls and roller rinks erupt from the ground overnight, thrusting up through meadows and plots of trees. Everywhere he looks there is another bookstore, another burger place, an arcade, a playground, a golf course, a hospital, a school, a supermarket, a bank, a church, a bowling alley, a nightclub, a car wash—but the truth is they have all been there for years, and Kevin has simply never noticed them.

Where has he been living all this time?

There are so many blocks, so many neighborhoods.

The van makes a quick series of turns before it stops at a house he has never seen. The street is quiet enough for him to hear the trees clicking, the grass rustling. A stop sign with a missing bolt clanks against its steel post. Only the cars parked along the curb suggest that the party has already started.

Kevin follows Ethan inside. From the TV Huey Lewis sings, "Don't need money, don't take fame, don't need no credit card to ride this train." A couple of seniors lie arm wrestling on the living room carpet, their torsos propped up on their massive elbows. Kevin's heart begins to race when he sees Kenneth in the corner, pouring a Pepsi from one of the two-liters on the card table, but it is some other guy, a lanky D&D type with his own striped button-up, his own brown hair, and oh thank God not Kenneth at all.

Ethan knows everyone, and Kevin knows Ethan, so no one asks him why he's there. And no one will, he figures, as long as the two of them remain where they are, standing against the wall swigging lukewarm Sprite from plastic cups. He feels the way he used to feel at the water fountain after recess, as if he could drink and drink without ever stopping, an open well with a body around it.

Sarah is sitting on the couch watching music videos, absent-mindedly toying with a scrunchie, her fingers lazily separating and then coming back together. Man. She is (1) unearthly, (2) unconceited, (3) unequaled, and (4) unattainable.

(5) Unfortunately.

He has liked her since he was six years old—half his life. He lets his eyes skip through the room. Some crazy screw-driver tightens his ribs around his heart. All the girls with their makeup and their hair spray. All the boyfriends with their girlfriends. It's not that no one loves him. That's not it at all. He is loved in a hundred little ways by a hundred different people. That should be enough, shouldn't it? But he can't stop wishing he was loved in one big way, by one person in particular.

It is terribly late to be in some strange grown-up's house. Ordinarily Kevin would have brushed his teeth and changed out of his school clothes by now. Gradually the party has developed the pleasant buzzing softness of an episode he is just lying in bed imagining.

At ten, the youth minister situates a folding chair in the middle of the living room and calls everyone together for a game. The rules: a volunteer sits blindfolded with his hands covering his ears while the game master devises three options—for instance a bear hug, a neck massage, and an Indian burn; one, two, and three. Then the volunteer removes his blindfold, picks a number, and selects someone to perform the mystery routine. "Are you ready? Let's play." A blond girl with black eyebrows listens to a guy serenade her with Phil Collins. A girl in stonewashed jeans gets her back scratched through her sweater. A tall guy in a letter jacket, with the little white bull's-eyes of recently removed braces on his teeth, accidentally chooses a noogie, and everyone whistles and claps and talks in a ripple of voices.

Kevin is not expecting the youth minister to say his name, or "Why don't you come up here and take yourself a turn, buddy?" but he does, so Kevin walks to the chair, slips the blindfold over his eyes, and listens to the stampede sound his palms make when he covers his ears. Then someone taps him on the shoulder, and he can hear again. He removes the blindfold. Through the window he sees the yellow glow of the porch light, reaching barely as far as the hedges.

"All right, Kevin. One, two, or three?"

He always says two.

"Great. And who's going to help you out with that?"

In his head he urges himself to reply, "I'm no fool, Sarah," but though he is ninety percent certain it would be a cool thing to say, he just points, says a crackling, "Her," and tries to prevent himself from smiling because if he smiles she will know everything. The *oooh* that stretches through the room makes his armpits go clammy. Sarah cuts slowly through the crowd. Then she is inches away, her face diving in to kiss him, and Thad and Kenneth can go to hell, because he is better, he is better, he is better.

. . . .

The locker room door opens in an aerosol of sweat and shampoo—*fwoosh*, all at once, a steamy summer day's worth— and Kevin makes a dash for his duffel bag.

"*And* he's off," Brandon Ostermueller says. "*Ándale! Ándale! Arriba!*"

No answer from Kevin. He veers past the lockers and skids up to the bench. He is already stretching his shirt off with his elbows. Everyone has a talent, and dressing out is his. The nimbleness of it, the zip—for him, undressing is like sprinting or shooting baskets: a sport. Back in December someone noticed he was always the first one to return to the mats after the whistle blew, and ever since, he has been changing faster and faster, trading his school clothes for his gym clothes like a frog hopping between puddles. Suddenly, mysteriously, he has developed a reputation. It belongs to him now. He feels obliged to maintain it. His shirt and his shoes and his jeans, *go, go, go*, then his white Mustang T-shirt and purple athletic shorts, *go*, then his shoes again, laced so loosely he is able to step back into them without jimmying at the heels, and in forty seconds he is out the door, *go*, leaving behind the white towels slung over the wooden benches, the long dicks hanging from nests of black hair, all the things that make him feel like a little kid.

He beats everyone else by at least a minute, sharing the big empty gym with Coach Dale, who coughs quietly, rattling his wristwatch as if it might be broken. "Kev my man, you need to slow down and smell the roses. You ever hear that expression?"

"No, Coach."

"It means you keep running so hard and you're gonna miss all the good stuff."

But that's not right. It's not right because the world is running as fast as he is. If he slows down he'll fall behind, and everything will rush away from him. The flowers will disappear in a million paint streaks of color.

Today the class is finishing up its hockey segment. "Let's go, folks," Coach says. "Let's go, let's go, come on, put some lead in it." He gives the whistle a shut-up blast, the kind that keeps lengthening out of itself in a single shrill note, then ends without so much as a flutter. He divides the class into teams and distributes the sticks. The grips are wrapped in padded white handlebar tape, and so are the blades, and thank God, because Craig Brooks has spent the past two weeks flailing at the ball from all directions, leaving checkmark-shaped bruises on everyone's legs. He keeps grunting, body-checking, and heaving his shoulders, punishing anyone who gets in his way. And in fact not a minute goes by before he hits the knob of Kevin's ankle with a hard downward chop, like a woodcutter splitting a log. Needles of pain rise to Kevin's knee. Enough, goddamn it, he decides, is enough. He waits for his moment, following the fray from one side of the gym to the other until a gap opens up and he can take aim at Craig's shin.

"Holy mother!"

Craig holds his fist to his neck and does a quick little hunched-over evangelist's walk: *And the Lord spoke to me, brothers and sisters, and in my darkest hour I heard His voice.*

At the end of class, in the locker room, he poses with his leg out behind him and complains, "Man, someone literally smacked the hell out of me back there. It was like *wham*, and I was like *Jesus*."

Kevin hides his smile inside his shirt as he changes. Thirty seconds and he has returned to his polo and his blue jeans. Another ten and he has stamped his feet back into his shoes. The concrete walls repay the slightest sound. Kevin always carries two bags to PE, his duffel bag for his gym clothes and his camera bag for his books. He stands by the exit with a bag on each shoulder, waiting for the 3:30 bell. The guys who shower are showering, and the guys who don't are spraying angel wings of deodorant under their arms, and Shane Wesson is thrashing the air with his hands, flinging his clothes left and right. "I'm," he gasps, "in," he gasps, "training," he says. "Better watch out, Brockmeier. I'm coming for you."

There is a part of himself that Kevin dislikes, some guy on a ladder who is constantly testing the rails for vibrations from below. "Give it your best shot."

"Oh, I will, little man. Trust me, this shit is on!"

"Yeah, sure, whatever, Shane."

And then, as always, the bell.

It is mid-February, homegoing week, which is like homecoming week on its way out the door—five days of spirit activities leading up to the final basketball game of the season. Thursday is the big one, the fun one, costume day, with a different assignment for every grade. The seniors are supposed to dress like seventh-graders, the seventh-graders like seniors. For more than a week now, Kevin has been putting together his outfit—blue jeans, shaded glasses, and a button-up shirt, along with a wig he has scissored down to a tight black chop and a can of shoe polish for his face, neck, and hands: Darnell Robertson. Darnell is the only black student at CAC, the coolest and most recognizable of all the seniors. People will know who Kevin is right away, no question. But there is a long strand of pep rallies and free-throw competitions to get through before Thursday, so his costume will have to wait.

That night there is spaghetti with garlic bread, and Prince and "Darling Nikki," and New Edition and "Cool It Now," and *TV's Bloopers & Practical Jokes*, and a geography chapter and a Choose Your Own Adventure book, and lights out at 10:30. Our Father, who art in Heaven, hallowed be thy name, thy kingdom come, thy will be done, on Earth as it is in Heaven.

On Tuesday, before English, Miss Vincent is in some weird hawk-mood. She sizes everyone up from her seat at the corner of her desk, swiveling her neck to watch them as they cross the room. Before the bell rings she announces that there won't be any classwork today. Instead they can play a game. "Any ideas?"

Kevin suggests the youth group game, but he has trouble describing the rules. "Okay, so there's a guy in charge, and there's a player. You sit in a chair and you cover your ears, and then you pick one, two, or three, and it's like one someone sings you a song, and two someone rubs your shoulders," and three Sarah Bell kisses you on the cheek—or no, the lips—a leisurely French kiss—and nobody else is there, and the room is so dark it's like you're both dreaming, and she stumbles, landing right on top of you, with her hands on your shoulders and her legs doubled together around your hips, pinning you down so that you can't move unless she lets you, and *why hello there.*

"And three maybe someone kicks you on the shin."

Tania Pickett coughs up a look. "Why would you want to be *kicked*?"

"It doesn't have to be a kick. Anything. It could be anything."

"Let's play a different game."

Miss Vincent suggests something called Laps. It's simple, she says: she'll ask a question, and if your answer is no, you'll keep your place, and if your answer is yes, you'll move to the next chair in line—maybe an empty seat, maybe a lap, maybe a whole stack of laps.

Does your first name start with a vowel? *No.*

Do you play a musical instrument? *No.*

Were you born here in Arkansas? *No.*

Have you studied for tomorrow's quiz? *Yes.*

Soon there are scattered chains of abandoned desks everywhere, along with a few stray clumps holding two people or three. By the big glowing courtyard painting of the window—all red bricks, white mortar, and blue sky—sits an isolated chair where the kids are banked five laps deep, like a caterpillar posed upright on a throne, an image so clear Kevin must have seen it in a picture book.

Have you ever flown in an airplane? *Yes.*

Do you know how to swim? *Yes.*

Do you know how to water-ski? *No.*

Have you ever seen *Casablanca*? *No.*

Have you ever visited another country? *No.*

Do you listen to Bruce Springsteen? *Yes.*

"Today," Miss Vincent asks, "right now, as we speak, are you wearing white underwear?"

And of course Kevin is, his usual Fruit of the Looms, but he's confident no one will put him to the test, and if he has to lie about it, then fine, no problem, he'll lie because Noelle Batch is sitting on his lap. He knows that if he were watching himself from across the room the way he watches the couples at the shopping mall, his limbs would practically tingle with his hunger to trade places. This kind of craving is so familiar that he has almost grown to like it. *My God, does that guy know how lucky he is? What Kevin wouldn't give to be him for a while!* Bodies begin shuffling like beads on an abacus, but Noelle doesn't move, so neither does he. A stillness settles over him as he waits for Miss Vincent to ask the next question.

"What color is *your* underwear, Kevin?"

Another night and another day and on Wednesday, after school, Bateman comes buzzing into Kevin's driveway on his moped and punches the horn. It is a sunlit winter afternoon, so peaceful that only the crowns of the trees are stirring. To the dogs across the street the engine noise seems to signal a calamity. *Danger! Danger! Warning!* they bark. They have never heard anything like it.

Bateman is (1) adventurous, (2) cheerful, (3) freckled, (4) independent, and (5) hilarious. Something about the way his voice rises into a joke and then stops dead, like a mountain climber calling it quits just before he reaches the peak, makes it impossible not to laugh at him. His freckles, he says, are the source of his power. He and Kevin have been friends since the second grade. So many years, so many jokes. Together on his moped they set out through Leawood to Hillcrest, where the new comics have just hit the racks at Gadzooks. Kevin balances himself on the back edge of the bike's seat pad, the metal frame vibrating beneath him like a washing machine. The sun sparks through the trees, and the wind makes a sputtering noise, and he traces the strands of tar on the road, their slender black lines railroading open and shut. "Feeling steady back there?" Bateman says. "Here, grab hold."

Kevin clings to his waist as they tilt around the corner. Sometimes people are fat beneath their clothing.

Grant, the Gadzooks guy, has ice-blue eyes, a silver necklace, and a beard that's mostly mustache. "You two gentlemen," he says, and he pistol-points at them, sorting through the boxes until he finds their names, then fanning their comics out on the counter like playing cards, "had some monthlies come in this afternoon." These days the store is reserving *X-Men*, *X-Factor*, and *West Coast Avengers* for Kevin, along with *Secret Wars II*, which is finishing its run, and the *Punisher* miniseries, which has just started. His total usually comes to something-ninety-eight or something-seventy-three. He likes to slide the pennies back to Grant with a casual keep-the-change, like a man in a suit at a bar.

Today, after looking over the new releases, Kevin picks his way through the junk chest. The comics there are three for a dollar and you never really know. Once, claims Grant, as an experiment, he tucked a mint-condition *Iron Man 1* in with all the *Dazzlers* and *Mad House Comics* to see if anyone would find it. No one did.

You never really know. Lately Kevin has been bothering himself with the idea that nothing is certain, nothing can be proven. Not one thing, not in all the world. The sun will rise tomorrow. *Prove it.* The sun rose this morning. *Prove it.* The sun is in the sky. *Prove it.* There's a sun at all. *Prove it.* The world is like a box of Kleenex, every doubt pulling another along behind it. You can always find a new reason to distrust the facts.

Kevin has been wondering if he shouldn't become a lawyer, but the last time he mentioned the idea, Bateman said, "So you keep telling me. Why's that again?"

"Because I like arguing. I'm good at it."

"You are?"

"Of course I am."

"Kevin, you can't just say prove it and expect to win cases. The phrase is reasonable doubt, not demented and annoying doubt."

He replays the conversation as he rummages through the comics. *Prove it. Demented and annoying. Prove it.* Is it just his imagination, or does the browning paper smell stronger in the winter than it did in the summer? He holds an old *Marvel Two-in-One* up to his nose and ruffles the pages. Woody, dusty, plastery. Like a scratch-and-sniff peanut sticker. Maybe there's a difference between how strong comics smell in the heat and how strong they smell in the air conditioning. It's a good idea for a science experiment.

I see what you mean now, Kevin. How could I have been so obstinate? This court pronounces the defendant innocent of all charges.

Bateman is clearly wrong, and Kevin is clearly right.

He pays for his monthlies at the register. This time, though,

Grant refuses to keep the change. "No, man, look, you gotta start taking your money with you. Hell if I'm gonna let you bump me into a higher tax bracket." That's how he talks, a grown-up among grown-ups. Kevin seals his comics in their Mylar bags and slips them into a brown paper sack, squaring the edges off so that he has a perfect little floppy rectangular package he can stow between his belt line and his coat. Plastic, paper, and cotton—three layers of wrapping. Bateman could lay his bike down in a skid of sparks, send it tumbling like a playground jack over the asphalt and the grass, and it wouldn't matter, Kevin thinks, his comics would be absolutely fine. Hell if the accident would even scour the gloss from the covers.

The two of them go dragonflying up Kavanaugh, accelerating over the hills and kicking at the pavement on the curves. By the time they reach Kevin's driveway, his mom is already home from work, his brother home from the creek or the playground. The place mats are set, the frying pan sizzling on the stove. For dinner there is Steak-umms and macaroni salad, and for TV there is *Highway to Heaven*, and then Kevin has gone to sleep and woken up, and it is finally Thursday, and he has locked himself in the bathroom, coloring his face and his neck, his hands and his arms, with the shoe polish his dad gave him for Christmas. The paste appears against his skin in raised streaks, blackish-brown bands that remind him of the currents of slush in a freezing river, cooler and denser than everything around them. He does his best to buff them smooth with a rag.

"Are you sticky?" his brother asks. "You look all, like, gummy."

"And you're absolutely sure you're *supposed* to dress like this," his mom says.

By the time he meets the carpoolers in his clothes and his wig, he has begun to wonder if the whole Darnell thing might not be a mistake. Will anyone else dress up? Will anyone actually know who he is? The shoe polish has been drying slowly through its range of browns. He's not sure his skin is even the right color anymore. What a bad idea.

He holds his breath and opens the carport door, forcing himself to conquer his nerves, and climbs into the backseat of the little red sports car Kenneth's mom drives. For a moment he feels as strange as he must look. Why does he keep taking school and transforming it into a *situation*? Inside himself he experiences a yanking sensation, as if someone has done that tablecloth trick and he has fallen without actually moving, his body clinking into place like silverware. Then Kenneth catches his eye in the mirror and says, "Oh—my—*God*, Kevin. Tell me you're not Darnell Robertson," and Kevin's makeup stiffens around his smile. He can't help himself. His entire life, whenever anyone has said his name, his feelings have flown shining right out of his face. *Kevin*, he hears, and he is like a baby in a playpen.

He answers the way he imagines Darnell would: "You know it, my man."

"Good Lord."

Plenty of other seventh-graders are wearing costumes, but it looks as if Kevin is the only one who's chosen a specific senior. In his classes there is no one else like him. He is like a fire or a mirror: everyone who sees him has to decide—do they turn toward him or away?

After Bible, in English, Miss Vincent leaves a tiny gap of air between the *mis-* and the *-ter* in "Mr. Brockmeier," like a dirt racer taking a ramp.

"That's me," says Kevin.

"Another semester, another costume, another meeting," she says.

"I don't get it."

"You keep creating these . . . predicaments. And the administration keeps talking them over."

"Well, yeah, see, it's homegoing week. The seniors are supposed to be seventh-graders, and the seventh-graders are supposed to be seniors. I'm Darnell."

One of her cheeks dimples. It is the opposite of an expression—an expression bricked up before it can escape.

Everything is a secret Kevin doesn't understand.

At lunch his friends won't stop pretending he's actually Darnell, the real thing, eighteen and ready to graduate, except for Leigh Cushman, who insists that Kevin looks more purple than black and keeps asking him if the milkshakes are ready.

"Look," Kevin says. "Does the Grimace wear glasses and a button-up shirt? No. Is the Grimace a senior at CAC? No. Does your joke make any sense at all?"

"Yes," Leigh says, and he tacks the table with his finger. This is what he does—decrees a joke again and again until it becomes funny.

Saul Strong, Mike Beaumont, Leigh Cushman, Sean Lanham, and James Dexter—Kevin has been eating with the same group of guys since Christmas. He would never ask any of them to spend the night, would never even call them on the phone because he doesn't know them well enough, hasn't known them long enough. But even if they aren't his *old* friends, they are still his friends. He considers the spot on the bench where he arranges his feet around the table's metal legs his own private corner of the lunchroom. Sometimes, if it's cold or if it's raining, Asa Stephens and Danny Morgan will join them, too, but today, though the sky is yellowing with clouds and the wind keeps making these great inhalations, a thousand of them one right after another, so that if the air had buttons they would have popped by now, Asa and Danny are eating outside, in the courtyard between the buildings, or maybe on the grass by the bluff.

"What brings you to the lunchroom at this hour, Darnell?"

"Tell me, Darnell, what are your plans for college?"

"How does it feel to be black, Darnell?"

"How does it feel to be purple, Grimace?"

"Can I touch your hair, Darnell?"

"Let me see your palms."

"Do you get tanned in the summer?"

"Wait," James Dexter asks, "has Darnell actually *seen* you yet?"

"I don't think so," Kevin says. "In chapel he was looking for someone in the bleachers, but as far as I know his eyes skipped right over me."

"I bet he's gonna kick your ass."

Someone accidentally jostles the door, and it swings halfway closed before the doorstop's rubber toe catches it.

"Don't laugh," James says. "I'm serious. I bet he's gonna kick your white ass."

Something washes through Kevin's face. He would be willing to bet he is blushing, even if no one can tell. He sees his life as an endless series of *but why*s. Thad says you're a liar. Kenneth isn't speaking to you. Sarah will never kiss you again—it was only an accident of circumstance that she kissed you in the first place. It's too late for you to become a different person. You'll never be tall, and you'll never be strong. You'll always run fastest when no one is watching. You're not our friend anymore. Your family is fucking strange. We want you to leave, right now. Leave, Kevin. I'm not kidding. Stickers are over. Mad Libs are over. Comics are over. That stuff is for fags. No one has liked that shit in years. They never will again. Nothing you love is going to last. It's impossible to rewind the grades on their spool, impossible to pause them, impossible to replay the good parts. Billy Joel isn't cool anymore—Mötley Crüe is. Mötley Crüe isn't cool anymore—Yngwie Malmsteen is. You're an idiot if you haven't heard of Yngwie Malmsteen. You can't walk around dressed like Dolly Parton. You can't walk around dressed like Darnell Robertson. Darnell is going to kick your white ass. But why?

He hardly knows Darnell, doubts Darnell has ever so much as spoken his name, but one of the other seniors must have told him about Kevin's costume, because half an hour later, in math, something in the room's attention shifts toward the door like a sheet of water listing across a pan. Kevin glances up to see Darnell at the window, staring hard at him from behind the gold frames of his glasses. Amazing how unobstructed a thought can be. *I'll be goddamned*, Darnell is thinking—not amused, not resentful, only intent. *I'll be goddamned*. Each word is so forceful and direct that Kevin would swear he is speaking out loud. Darnell flattens his fingertips against the window like some sea creature testing the glass of an aquarium. Then he notices the roomful of people watching him and allows his expression to twist. He spotlights Kevin with his eyes, mugging for a laugh. *I can't believe this crazy shit I'm seeing.* That's what his face says now, but it's an act, a routine. Whatever he is genuinely thinking has vanished into the privacy of his mind and drawn the darkness around it.

Mrs. Dial laughs along with the others. She tries to make a joke, "Should I ask our friend if he has a hall pass?"

But the window is suddenly empty, and the water spills back across the pan, and for the rest of the period, bent to their worksheets or sharpening their pencils, everyone keeps cocking their heads to see what Kevin is doing. He loves it. Darnell is the star, Kevin the co-star, and what could be better, he wonders, what could be better? Switch off a TV and its screen will bloom with static electricity, a strange soft force field of it that scatters at your touch. That's how he feels: you could swipe your palms over him, and his skin would sizzle audibly into the air. The tingle covers him from head to toe. It lasts deep into SRA, melting away only after Mrs. Bissard hands out a pop quiz and his head fills with trues and falses.

An hour later, on his way to PE, he is passing Miss Vincent's door when she calls out, "Good news, Mr. B. You're off the hook."

He back-steps and says what he always does: "Absolutely."

He's not sure when it started, this *absolutely* phase of his. Weeks ago? Months? All he knows is that it has the broken-in feel of a word he has been using forever. A few weekends ago, for an hour or two, just to annoy him, his brother began echoing every *absolutely* of Kevin's with an *absolutely* of his own.

Only then did he realize how frequently he has been resort-
ing to it. Surely if he tried he could strip it from his vocabu-
lary, he thought, but instead he has adopted it, consciously
and officially. It is his answer to everything now, whether
he understands it or not. He likes the way it rolls off his
tongue—*absolutely*, BUM-buh-BUM-buh—like a child skip-
ping along the sidewalk.

"So," continues Miss Vincent, "you can consider your situation resolved."

He has to hurry. PE is on the other side of the school. "Yeah.
Absolutely. Resolved."

She should be smoking. When she laughs, the sound should
puff from her nostrils in three separate bursts of white. "All
right then, Kevin, I'll see you tomorrow. Cosmetics-free, I
trust."

In the gym Shane Wesson is limbering himself up against
the bleachers. "This," he warns Kevin, "is the day," and he
grunts, stretching his hamstrings, "you go down, my friend.
You think you can dress out? You can't dress out. We'll see
who can dress out in here."

"Dressing out—please," Kevin says, but he is faking. He
knows the contest isn't real, knows he shouldn't care, but
he can't help it, he does. Somewhere inside him stands a
hyperactive little guardian-figure, squeaking with anger and
waving a hamburger sword, protecting any small thing he
believes Kevin has gained, no matter how trivial. It's probably this zeal of his, this inability to shrug his shoulders and
say *whatever*, that inspires Kevin's friends to race him to the
counter, to challenge him for the shotgun seat, to mess with
him. Once, in first grade, Thad asked him how he had learned

to run so quickly, and Kevin told him that he practiced by sprinting twenty times around the house every day—a total lie. He was fast back then, that's all, a Corvette going sixty on the highway. His speed belonged to him and him alone. Thad couldn't have it. No one could.

Coach Dale arrives in his shirt and tie. Name by name he works his way through the alphabet, from Joseph Arendt to Jake Grundon, Steve Mollette to Barry Robertson. Shane inches to the edge of the bleachers, flexing the sole of his high-top against the polished wooden riser. It is the closest he can come to an on-your-mark stance while sitting down. As far as Kevin can tell, he does it without attracting an atom of attention.

It is raining now, hard, and a thunderclap detonates across the sky, leaving smaller and smaller rumbles behind it until no one could guess what they are the thunder or the rain or just some flaw in the gym's lighting.

"All right, kiddos," their other coach, Coach Strand, says. "We were going to have you run the loop today, but that's out, for obvious reasons, so what we've got for you is some indoor calisthenics. Gonna get those little hearts pumping."

At the sound of the whistle, Shane uses his long legs to outpace Kevin to the locker room. By the time the rest of the class gets there, he has already whipped off his belt and started on his shoelaces, but it is a pretty dinky head start, and in ten seconds flat Kevin has caught up with him, trading his shoes and his jeans for his gym shorts and his shoes again.

There's no time to unbutton his shirt, so he yanks it over his head. His wig and his Darnell glasses—he had forgotten he was wearing them—fly pinging into the wall like bobby pins. He is in the lead now, but Shane is right behind him, and for once everyone cares, or at least pretends to. Shane Roper of all people—Mr. Sarcasm—starts chanting, "Go, go, go," and in all likelihood he is just doing it to amuse himself, but a few of the others join in, Joseph Rimmer and Matthew Connerly and even Kenneth and Thad, and Kevin can feel his whole body responding to the chant, his nerves hurrying him on, and *I'm off the hook*, he thinks, *I'm off the hook*, and what in the world does that mean?

He has never noticed how short the sleeves of his T-shirt are. The hems barely touch his biceps. Immediately above his wrists are two ragged lines where the shoe polish fades into unpainted skin. Beneath the humming blue fluorescents of the locker room his hands look unusually brown, his arms unusually white.

Shane is still tying his shoes—a mistake: wasting time with shoelaces—when Kevin finishes dressing, smacks the door-frame, and shoots off for the gym. The basketball court is empty, hangarlike. Neither of the coaches is anywhere to be seen.

He reaches the purple-and-gold mat Velcroed to the wall behind the hoop, and "Yes!" he shouts. "Hwuh! In your face!" And maybe this will explain it: the rafters don't absorb his voice but instead widen it, strengthen it, so that it takes on the shape of the room. He feels as big as the gym, as big as the school. He is not a normal person anymore. He could be Giant-Man or Galactus, the Rock Biter with his good strong hands, a senior getting ready to graduate and go to college, to meet a girl and get married, to stride out into his life.

Not Darnell maybe, but someone like him.

Most Spirited.

Best Smile.

By 3:30, when the station wagon arrives, Kevin fits inside himself again, but his heart is still galloping, the rain still falling loud and heavy. The car goes plowing through the lake that forms where Bridgeway meets Crystal Hill Road. Then it braves the torrent of the highway, the windshield blurring and clearing, blurring and clearing. He finds the rhythm of the wipers oddly soothing, a strange kind of machine music. At home he takes a Little Hug and a Peanut Butter Bopper and settles into one of the lawn chairs on the back porch. He fixes his gaze on the corrugated plastic roof, where the water draws braided gray strings along the ribs. The rain striking the fiberglass sounds like fingers snapping. He can see it boiling in a thousand tiny circles. His face feels tight enough to crack.

. . . .

Jell-O Pudding Pops that preserve the wavelike peaked shape of your lips. Little Debbie Fudge Brownies that break in half along a groove in the frosting. Summer sausages like #2 pencils, cling-wrapped together on a Styrofoam platter. Strawberry Fruit Wrinkles that scent your fingers if you don't pour them directly into your mouth. Squares of American cheese sealed so tightly their wrappers show little pale lagoons of trapped air. Chocolate Pop-Tarts sprinkled with shards of something that tastes like sugar but looks like rock salt. Doo Dads floured with cheddar, great masses of leftover peanuts hiding at the bottom of the bag. Little Debbie Nutty Bars, two per wrapper, their sides pasted so lightly together that they separate with the sound bath bubbles make when you whisk through them with your finger. Monster Pops popsicles in three different styles—Satan holding a pitchfork, Frankenstein clutching a skull, and Dracula grasping his chest with eight riblike fingers—made with the kind of ice that splits apart in chunks rather than sunbursting loose from the stick in layers. Blueberry Toaster Strudels with snake trails of sticky icing. Crystal Light powder in frosted plastic tubs. Bon Bons ice cream nuggets in bells of melting chocolate. Capri Sun pouches you can reinflate once they're empty, squeezing the bottom to launch the stiff little arrow of the straw across the room. Bugles corn treats that you eat in fives—that *everyone* eats in fives—using them to make lion's claws or witch's fingers before you suction them loose with your lips: *hwoot, hwoot, hwoot, hwoot, hwoot.* Little Debbie Pecan Spinwheels and Little Debbie Swiss Rolls and Little Debbie Star Crunches and Little Debbie Oatmeal Creme Pies.

Usually Kevin marauds through the snacks as soon as he gets home from school, stuffing himself in his room, but today is different. Today he is on a reconnaissance mission. He taps his way slowly through the cabinets and the refrigerator, studying the possibilities box by box. The granola bars. The Fruit Roll-Ups. Someone at school has been stealing people's lunches from their lockers—including, for the fifth time now, his. He needs a new plan, since obviously the potato chips didn't work. That was his tactic on Monday, shaking a bunch of Ruffles into a clear plastic sandwich bag and then rigging the packet with a mousetrap, the snap kind, with a hook and a bar and a coil. In the morning, before first period, he tucked the chips into a brown paper sack and used them to booby-trap his locker. By noon, when the bell rang, the sack had fallen over, and there were shards of Ruffles everywhere. Which meant that the thief must have popped the door open, taking Kevin's lunch by the edges, and "Sweet," the guy had thought, "Score," but before he could make his getaway, the trap had sprung, showering him with potato chips—a *chips-plosion.* And out loud he had said, "Holy shit!" And the bar had caught the tip of his finger, and he had panicked and wrenched his hand loose, dropping the sack into Kevin's locker before he slammed the door shut, gave a quick glance

KEVIN BROCKMEIER

left and right, and went spurting off down the hallway. And for the rest of the day his friends had asked him, "Why do you keep sucking on your finger, man? You look retarded." And when he showed them the crack in his nail, and the sealed plane of beet-colored blood, they cringed and said, "Ah sweet *Ho*ly Christ, what'd a car door get you or something?"

Except that it must not have happened that way. If it had, Kevin's lunch wouldn't have been stolen again.

He wrings the last few drops from the fantasy.

That looks gruesome, man.

Dude, you should go to the office with that thing.

Now what did you do to yourself again?

The open refrigerator hums, shudders, and gives off a cut-grass smell. The grapes and the apples, the ketchup and mustard, sit there sharp and bright, throwing their colors out at him, as if it is always noon inside the refrigerator, on April the third, and everything is drenched in sunlight. It is hard to tell sometimes whether he is hungry or just plain bored.

A snack equals one Pop-Tart, one popsicle, or one Dixie cup full of Doo Dads or Bugles, though occasionally, when no one else is home, he will cheat and have two.

That evening, after TV, he does his geography, then lies on his back clutching Percy to his stomach. After which comes the part where Percy decides whether or not to muscle free of him. He lowers his ears, rearranges his weight, and stiffens his spine, then jumps a little invisible hurdle and trots from the room purring.

The dishwasher is bathing the dishes. The VCR is playing *All My Children*. The sound of a car decelerating around the curve reminds Kevin of Thad for some odd reason—how, when he used to spend the night, Kevin's mom would drop them off at Breckenridge and they would pocket the money she gave them for the movies, striding off into the yellow-lit darkness to hang out with girls. The shopping center's walk-ways were framed with X-shaped wooden beams, and Kevin would lounge in the fork of one looking cool, keeping his left leg rigid and letting his right dangle like a cat's tail, and beneath him, on the ground, Thad would take whichever girl he had picked to be his girlfriend and wrap her in kisses, and the trees would rustle in the wind, and the beetles would pankle against the lightbulbs, and it seems to Kevin that he was more grown-up on those chilly Friday nights than he has ever been since. He had a different best friend then, a differ-ent school, and though he didn't know it, he was at the peak of something.

Who can say what possesses him, but hardly a minute passes before he is calling Thad to ask if he wants to sleep over on Friday. Why shouldn't his life turn the other way for once? Why can't things go backward?

Thad seems guarded, suspicious, as if he is anticipating a prank. "Yeah? What do you want?"

"I was calling to see if maybe you can spend the night this weekend. Maybe Friday? After school?"

A T-shirty, smothered sound, a little hum of noise, and then, "Mom says I have to ask Dad, and Dad's not home. I'll let you know tomorrow, good?"

"That's cool. It's casual."

"Yeah. Right. 'Casual.'"

"I thought we could hang out at Breckenridge if you want. You know. 'See a movie.'"

"Uh-huh."

"Or go to the mall."

"Yeah, look, I've gotta go, so—bye."

Kevin is already singing Chicago's "Stay the Night" by the time he hangs up. He fixes his upper lip flat against his teeth like Peter Cetera, trying for that pulled-taffy voice of his. The words slide right out of him: "No need to hit me with an attitude, because I haven't got the time." He has the kind of brain that unearths songs all day long, one after another, harvesting them from books, movies, sermons, lessons, conversations, and announcements. The slightest scrap or echo of a lyric and *boom!*—there he'll be, reconstructing some twice-heard melody, verse, chorus, and verse. He does it with so little thought that sometimes he'll find himself hours deep in a song with no idea where it began. This time, though, the source is unmistakable. *Spend the night*, so *stay the night.*

Back in his room he runs his fingers down the rows of his tape box. Chicago is sandwiched between Van Halen and John Cougar Mellencamp. Funny how their titles sound like a quarterback calling hike: *19! 84! 17! Uh! Huh!*

More than half of Kevin's tapes are music club releases, six for the price of one from RCA or eleven for a penny from Columbia House. Every time he resurrects his membership, another big rattling cardboard brick of them will appear in his mailbox. Music club tapes are a bleached white plastic like candle wax, with a smell totally unlike the fruit-sugar scent of the tapes he buys from Target or Camelot, the see-through kind with the frosted lettering. He plugs *Chicago 17* into his stereo and rewinds it to the beginning. He has just enough time to listen to side one before he has to change for bed.

He goes to sleep with no plans, no ideas, yet locked in his mind the next morning is a strategy for revenge. No one's going to steal *his* lunch. He wakes like an athlete diving into cold water, with the same breath of excitement he remembers experiencing as a kid on Saturdays. There is a deadness to the house, a tingling moon-quiet. He feels as if he is somewhere he has never been, separated from the curving streets and grassy slopes of his neighborhood by light-years and miles—whole mountains away, whole galaxies away.

At first he is sorry to disturb the stillness, but then he hears the tick of the water heater as his mom turns on the shower, hears Percy scratching at the litter box, and instantly he is back home again. He pads to the kitchen to begin his work. Step one he makes a bologna-and-cheese sandwich. Step two he takes the top slice of bread, the undressed slice, into the bathroom, and pinches hold of the corner to douse it in urine. Step three: he bakes the bread dry with a hair dryer—it stiffens weirdly in the heat without ever quite toasting. And finally, step four: he writes "I peed on this sandwich" on a scrap of paper and plants it between the cheese and the lettuce.

He bags the sandwich up and takes it to school. The problem is that none of the lockers at CAC have real locks, just latches that slide open with a hard steel *chock*. What they are is *un*lockers. Take-what-you-wanters. Welcome-on-iners. The idea seems to be that since stealing is unchristian, Christians won't steal. Some theory. Kevin loads the morning's books into his camera bag, then puts his lunch on the backpack shelf—*so long, you, and good luck*—and cuts through the gym. Stretched out behind the basketball court is the stage the school uses for concerts and plays. It's a strange thing, that stage, able to fire pins and needles into him just by existing. Its curtains bulge and deflate in the air-conditioning. The lights turn to fuzz on its polished boards. If his life were a TV show, he thinks, it would be an episode of *Amazing Stories*, and the twist would be that the stage was actually alive. The stage has plans, he imagines. The stage knows what it wants. It wants to maneuver him up one of its skinny sunken mini-staircases, giving him intangible little bumps and plucks with its intangible little fingers. It wants him to put on a show. Butterflies: that's the nervous feeling you get in your stomach before a performance. But what do you call it when the performance is entirely in your imagination? Caterpillars maybe. Moths.

The first bell rings while he is still at half-court. By the time he reaches Bible, Thad has already claimed his seat. Kevin tries to attract his attention, but something else keeps catching his eye, something just to the right or the left, flea-hopping away whenever Kevin moves in for an interception.

Thad is asking Brandon—Drale, not Ostermueller—about a movie they both saw on TV. "Did you watch the Showtime version or the USA version?"

"USA. Why? What's the difference?"

"R versus PG. You know that massage scene where chick thinks dude's a girl?"

"Ooohhh yeah."

"You gotta see the Showtime version. That's all I'm gonna say."

Thad fiddles with his gold chain, triggering the clasp *click click click*. Not until Mr. Garland has taken roll does Kevin finally manage to signal him. He mouths "Friday?" and Thad creases his brow and mouths back "What." Then he makes a revolving-door motion with his finger—*turn the other way*—and just like that Kevin remembers that they are no longer friends.

Of course. He is such a kid. It kills him that their days of kicking the soccer ball around are over, kills him that he never knew how little it would take to smash them. Nothing. Nothing. A split second. A white lie. In his memory he hears *Cut it out, guys,* and *Detective La,* and suddenly he feels the blur of heat in his eyes. He hopes no one sees him, though he would bet a hundred dollars they do. Sometimes his feelings run so hard in him he's sure they must pour from his skin. And sometimes he's surprised that other people notice him at all.

An hour later, for instance, in English, Miss Vincent reads the class a story and "The End," she says. "Show of hands. Who's an ant *annnnd*—who's a grasshopper? Kevin! A grasshopper! Why's that?"

Clearly the ant should have shared his food—that's what Kevin thinks, and he says so. He has a way of taking an answer and, without hammering or tugging at it, making it sound like an election speech. After he has finished talking, he notices Lisa Minton staring at him from across the circle of desks, slouching so low in her chair that the shoulders of her jacket engulf her neck. She is puzzled enough to ignore the silence of the room and ask, "What's it about that you're crying all the time?"

He realizes that he is still sniffing and blinking. "I'm not sure." The truth is that he always thought he would outgrow it.

"Do you have like allergies?"

"Bee stings."

"No, I mean like pets or dust or pollen."

"I don't know. I don't think so."

"Are you sick then?"

"Let's talk about something else."

"Yes," Miss Vincent agrees. "Let's," and because she laughs, everyone else does, too.

Someone's footsteps go beating down the hallway like an Indian drum. How it works who knows, but all of a sudden Kevin imagines his locker door springing open with a pop and a shiver. His palms begin to sweat. There are two things happening today—Thad and the sandwich—and if one of them doesn't go right, he thinks, surely the other will. He spends the next few hours concentrating just hard enough to do his work. After science and before geography, the brown paper bag is right where he left it, but forty-five minutes go by, and when he joins the lunch crowds, it is gone—snatched! He gives his locker a triumphant smack. His throat makes a crowlike cackle. It is unlike any sound he has ever heard himself produce. Walking past the classrooms and the bulletin boards, he feels a wonderful lifting sensation, as if space has flip-flopped around him and a whole world of things are rising that should be falling. Someday this is how he will die, he imagines, so full of happiness he will burst from his life a rocket.

He finds a seat next to Ethan Carpenter, who plunges straight into Bill Cosby's Lone Ranger bit. "Tonto, go to town," he says, and "Kemosabe, go to Hell," Kevin answers. It is the best and most foul-mouthed line on the record, and then "All right," Kevin says, scouting around the lunchroom. He doesn't want anyone to overhear them. "Listen to this."

Right away Ethan begins struggling against his face. He

compresses a smile into the far corner of his mouth, shakes his head, and releases a few coughlike sounds of amusement.

"Dude," he says at the end of Kevin's story, "that's disgusting."

"Yeah, I'm so proud."

"Do you think someone actually ate it?"

"Of course."

"Dude," again, "that's disgusting. Who do you think it was?"

Christian Gann is unwrapping one of the little square burgers from the vending machine. Randy Garrett is widening his lips around a Funyun. Everyone is a suspect.

"Actually—" The first lunch starts at 11:50, the second at 12:40, with twenty-five minutes of overlapping class time in between. "I bet it was one of the older guys. I'm gonna say it's still waiting in the bag to be eaten. Just   you know—fuming in there."

"You're sick."

"Stewing."

"Gross."

"But not for long."

The faculty lounge squares out into the room like an aquarium. The way the teachers drift around behind the flatness of the windows, forming quiet shapes with their mouths, makes it easy to believe they can't hear anything, but when some ninth-graders start jostling one of the snack machines to unsnag a bag of chips, Principal McCallum opens the door and says, "Come on now, fellas. Calm down."

Scrape the skin from his voice and you'll always find an implied *for Pete's sake.*

"I can guarantee one thing," Ethan says to Kevin.

"What's that?"

"Nobody'll want to eat your lunch again after today. Not even you."

"Actually I'm kind of starving."

Ethan slides him a Tupperware bowl of green grapes. "Knock yourself out." Some of the grapes are still bunched together. Kevin loves the tiny *snikt* of separation they make as he plucks them loose from their stems.

He is picking a bit of wood from his tongue when Kenneth comes flowing over and drapes an arm around his shoulders. "Kevin my friend! I've got a question for you. Why did you ask Thad to spend the night?"

A voice on one side of him and a hand on the other, and instinctively Kevin pivots toward the hand. Thad and his gang are a few tables away, Shane and Clint and the others, their eyes razoring directly in on him. They look the way people in movies do when their minds belong to someone else—like clones, things from outer space, brainwashees. All this time they must have been wondering what they could force him to say. He can practically re-create the whole scenario: Thad telling them about the phone call, then suggesting, "Do you know what would be hilarious? If we went over and asked guy about it," and someone else adding, "Oh, I bet he'll do that blinking thing he does," and Kenneth volunteering, "I don't care. What the hell. I'll go."

Now he sinks his weight onto his arm and says, "Let me rephrase. Why did you call Thad last night? Had him on your mind, did you?"

"I don't know. Obviously it was a bad idea."

Suddenly Kenneth's tone softens. "Hey there. No need to get upset. We're just curious, that's all."

By some miracle Kevin controls his face. Just like that, though, his hunger dematerializes, and his feeling of victory fades away. He is himself all over again. He stands and says, "Thanks for the grapes, Ethan." The echo of it rises from the other table: *thanks for the grapes, grapes, thanks for the grapes*. Who knew that *grapes* was such a funny word? It is news to him.

He brushes past Stacey Leavitt, who is unzipping her jacket in the doorway. If she notices him, it is only as a blur of clothing, some white shoes and some plaid sleeves, the smell of soap or deodorant, whatever it is he smells like. He remembers that time, years ago, at recess, when he accidentally kicked her soccer ball into the street just as a semi came monstering through the intersection, and they all listened as it flattened the ball and then flattened it again in the notch between its immense rear tires. It would never have occurred to him that something could pop more than once.

Last week in science Mr. Garland told them that atoms are mostly empty space—ninety-nine-and-a-bunch-of-repeating-nines' worth—nothing but fleeting waves of energy and force attracting and repulsing each other. The universe is a sink-hole, the universe is a tube slide. It is the kind of day where Kevin feels as if he might slip through the vacuum of the ground and never stop falling.

In SRA, Chuck Carnahan sits behind him poking the back of his head with a pencil, leaving small silver indentations on his scalp. Kevin pretends not to notice, which makes Chuck laugh. It is a game, a joke, one they are playing together, as if Kevin's head is all leather and bone and he has no nerves whatsoever. Mrs. Bissard busies herself at the chalkboard. You can do anything you want in her class as long as you do it quietly. After six or seven thrusts, Kevin hears Chuck say, "Matthew. Matthew. Check this out," and *peck peck peck*, he goes. Kevin sits stone still. The crazy part is that he doesn't mind. He would find it hard to explain why Kenneth whispering so nicely to him is spiteful while Chuck jabbing him with a pencil is friendly, but that's the situation.

Two bells later and the day is almost over. He sits on the bleachers waiting for PE to start. He can still feel the marks on his skull, exotic darts of sensation that keep sparking off into numbness and then re-erupting. Is he hurt? he wonders. Are they real? Maybe your skin simply tingles a certain way if you pay enough attention to it. That's probably it, he decides, because as soon as Coach Dale blows his whistle to send everyone to the locker room, the twinges seem to stop. Kevin is at the front of the herd, rushing past the seniors benching weights and studying their veins in the mirrors, their skin salts wafting into the hallway. Until now he had no idea how badly he wanted to run, to throw off his clothes and change into his T-shirt and shorts. The last few kids have barely reached the benches, and already he is nearly dressed out. He has been getting faster and faster. These days no one can touch him. Twenty, thirty seconds and *wh-shaw!*—he is done.

The other coach, Coach Strand, comes roostering through the door to say, "Cease and desist, folks. Class meeting in the weight room. Come on Boothby, come on Cushman, don't just stand there lolling around with your arms hanging—hustle!"

Kevin stomps back into his shoes before following the others outside. He is like a magician whose big instantaneous trick is to enter a cabinet wearing one color and exit wearing another. The seniors can scarcely believe it. He isn't sure which of them says, "Nuh-*uh*," and which, "No way. You can't change that fast. That's impossible," only that for a moment, in his tiny way, he is famous.

The class is halfway through its wrestling unit. Yesterday they finished practicing holds and throws, and today my friends, today compadres, they are actually going to fight. The meeting is about the President's Physical Fitness Test, the results for which have finally arrived, and as soon as it is over and everyone has dressed, they gather at the far wall of the basketball court, where they unstitch the mats from their Velcro bands and heft them onto the floor. They land heavily, sending a great smack of air into the room. With a noise like that, you know that something has happened.

In a few weeks, right here in the gym, CAC will be hosting a lock-in. Kevin can't get over it—how this very space, buzzing with exercise and light, will be blanketed in darkness, filled with hundreds of girls and hundreds of guys swimming in a giant sea of sleeping bags. Turn the lights off and there's nothing that can't be different. Maybe Kevin will find a girlfriend. Ann Harold will whisper, "Over here, you." Noelle Batch will mistake him for someone else. Sarah Bell will tow him off by the wrist and fall in love with him.

It is time for the lightning tournament, and gradually, two by two, the other featherweights in the class end up clapped together on the mat: Sean Hammons and Caleb Kellybrew, Jim Boothby and Mike Beaumont, Matthew Sesser and Peter Vickerel. As soon as one fighter pins another, the coaches call the match with a "Rimmer!" or an "Arendt!" and select the next pair. Name by name the roster dwindles. Matthew LeDoux. Sean Lanham. Randy Garrett. Michael Berridge.

Kevin stands on the sidelines watching the Twister-shapes
they make out of their bodies. Levon Dollard. Shane Roper.
William Carpenter. James Dexter. And there goes the last of
the small kids. Ethan Carpenter. Thad Brooks. Barry Robertson. Adrian Phipps.

Kevin knows it is going to happen and then it does. A
prickling feeling chases itself up his legs, until suddenly, with
a celebratory little rising drawl, Coach Strand says, "Last
round. Brockmeier! Grundon! You're up."

Of course everyone laughs. Kevin is as thin as a paint-
brush, at most eighty-four or eighty-five lubbs—why isn't it
pronounced that way?—while Jake Grundon looks the way
his name sounds: swollen to the stitches with muscle.

Ordinarily in PE Kevin tries to mouse around without
being noticed. Oh sure, he lets himself flash into view in the
locker room, but as soon as the athletic stuff starts, he does
his best to vanish again. A few weeks ago, during a game of
bombardment, he managed to shrink and fade and hush his
way into becoming the last surviving member of his team.
Balls have always seemed like missiles to him, flying fast
and hard. Not tools. Not playthings. Weapons. By the ordinary logic of sports he simply doesn't matter. He is narrow,
though—wily—and that day, as the clock ticked out its circles, he was able to dodge throw after throw with a quick
twist of his arms or hips. When the other team strung themselves along the line and coordinated their attack—"On the
count of three we aim all at once, understood? One, two,
three"—he dropped flat and the barrage bounced off the wall
above him. There was a popcorn of drumming, and a few of
the balls leapt out of bounds. He was so surprised to be alive
that he actually laughed out loud.

The trouble is that wrestling takes more than cunning. It takes leverage, muscle, and Kevin is nothing but scrawn, so skinny you could lay his forearm on a table and roll a marble down the tendons.

He decides to treat the match like a joke. Surely that's what the coaches are expecting. Why else would they pair him with a bulldozer like Jake Grundon?

He walks to the edge of the mat and gives Jake the death-finger. Then he rolls his neck until the joints crack. "Neutral positions," Coach Dale announces. "Readyyy—" The moment the whistle *fweets*, Kevin lowers his head and charges at Jake like a bull. Jake bends over, takes him by the ankles from behind, flips him upside down, and drops him on his head.

Coach Strand winces. "All right, Jake. None of that André the Giant stuff."

"Sorry, Coach."

Jake falls to his knees, and his palms staple Kevin's collarbones to the mat. Kevin bucks his legs, but it is like trying to flip a sack of cement off his shoulders: useless. Coach Dale counts down the seconds, and then "Match to Grundon!" he says. He gives a muffled clap, as if he is wearing cotton gloves. "Good try. Good try. Shake it off, Kev."

Kevin would rather have won, he can't deny it, but losing and losing badly brings with it a perverse feeling of accomplishment. Dead last is better than the middle of the pack. Dead last is a kind of second place. The excitement of the match lingers in his body, a fizz of nervous adrenaline that persists through the final bell and the long car ride over the river.

He doesn't realize he is sore until he has unlocked the kitchen door and deposited his books on the counter. He writes his name in the condensation on a Big K bottle: *K* is for *Kevin*. He feeds Percy a handful of Bonkers: Hello, cat. Then something in his head begins to float, and he crashes onto the sofa. The refrigerator makes a ticking sound. He is so glad to be home. He has sixteen hours until school starts.

Probably he will never know who ate the sandwich.

Probably Thad will never spend the night with him.

But the kitchen is next to the living room, and the bedrooms are lined up one-two-three, and the sunshine paints the shapes of the doors onto the hall. Here beneath these rooms it is solid ground all the way to the bottom of the universe.

. . . .

"'Which one of the letters does not belong in the following series? A—D—G—I—J—M—P—or—S'?"

"I have no idea. *G*?"

"No, *I*. It goes one letter on, then two off, then one on, then two off. A—b-c—D—e-f—G. Like that. Okay, how about '"If some Smaugs are Thors and some Thors are Thrains, then some Smaugs are definitely Thrains." This statement is true, false, or neither'?"

"I'm gonna say neither."

"Nope. False."

"But how do you know that?"

"The important word is *definitely*. *Maybe* some Smaugs are Thrains—not *definitely*. It could be that the only Thors that are Thrains are the ones that aren't Smaugs."

"Okay. Fine. Are we almost done?"

"Actually, that's it. The last question. So, let's see, you got twenty-eight—plus one, two—thirty correct, which means your IQ is . . . ninety-six. And that makes you . . . average."

Kevin is barely friends with Sean Hammons, and to be here at his house, in the weird incense of his family's cooking, on the couch that preserves the curves and valleys of their bodies, is bizarre. Not half as bizarre, though, as quizzing his mom with the IQ test he bought at B. Dalton last week. In her eyes Kevin catches a waspy look, a quick slant of anger. And you know what? She's right. The test is hard. He could swear that some of the questions have multiple correct answers. Take the one with the five pictures—no words, just illustrations—(a) a saw, (b) a knife, (c) a spoon, (d) a shovel, and (e) a screwdriver. And "Which one of the five is least like the other four?" At first Kevin guessed (e) the screwdriver, because it joins things together, while saws, knives, spoons, and shovels all take things apart, but the proper answer was (b) the knife, since *knife* starts with a *k* and the other four start with an *s*. But what if the knife was a steak knife—*s*? Or the saw was a handsaw—*h*? What if the issue was whether the object in the picture sloped this way or that way? Or whether it could be used as a murder weapon? It's tricky, a question like that.

From the driveway comes a crackle of broken concrete. At a distance it sounds the way potato chips sound when you're chewing. Mrs. Hammons glances outside and says, "Well hey, I think that's gotta be your mom's Subaru. And your bag's right there in the corner. And don't forget your poster boards."

"I won't."

Sean lives in an area of Little Rock that Kevin has never visited before, a tiny hidden drawer of a place, so far from the hills and curves of Northwick Court that even the spacing between the trees seems strange. The grown-ups say their hellos on the front porch, pretending to laugh about the things that grown-ups pretend to laugh about. Then the car closes its doors, and the house closes its, and Sean and his mom vanish back into the bricks and the carpet, and Kevin and his mom drive away together, mazing through the side streets that never quite intersect with the highway.

Barely three weeks of school remain: the last week of April and the first two weeks of May, plus Friday—tomorrow—a clean little pocket of woodsy air waiting to rush like a deep breath into everyone's lungs. The walkathon will start after lunch, the lock-in as soon as the final bell rings. But the centerpiece of the night will be the lip-synching contest. Kevin is practically sure of it. To win, he and Sean will need a gimmick, like that guy from *Puttin' on the Hits* who split himself into Diana Ross and Lionel Richie, painting his face two different shades of black.

"Hot for Teacher": that will be their song. They're going to serenade the Magic Marker drawing they made of Miss Vincent, all tall and hourglassy, with a red swimsuit, bunny ears, and crisscross stockings. The two of them used up the first part of the afternoon kneeling over a couple of poster boards, darkening her lines and then filling in the colors. They couldn't remember whether her eyes were blue or green or some watercolor in-between shade, so they flipped a quarter to decide. The second part they spent in Sean's backyard, listening to the song, then rewinding it and listening again. At first their moves were sloppy, embarrassing. Sean kept sawing around like Eddie Van Halen with his tennis-racket guitar, doing his impression of a virtuoso making the notes blur—*DOWnannanaDOWnannanaNOW*. Maddening. But Kevin insisted that they rehearse their choreography until they got it down pat: "Okay, I'll go over here and sing, 'I brought my pencil,' and then you can go over there and sing, 'Give me something to write on, man.' Ready? Let's try it."

"Wait, so do I go right or left?"

Still, as late as seventh grade, Kevin can't remember which is which. They should be immovable, he has always thought, like the Golden Gate Bridge and the Statue of Liberty. What was it Coach Dale taught them about how to read a map? *West is weft.* Kevin envisioned the United States in midair. "Left," he said.

"Gotcha." Sean pierced the strings of his guitar with his index finger and gave it a wobbly spin. "Left."

"So are you ready? We need this thing to be perfect if we're going to win. You're not going to pull another Case-of-the-Missing-Miss-Vincent on me, are you?"

"No. Jeez. I'll *be* there. How many times do I have to apologize?"

The power lines at the corner of Sean's roof opened out over the grass, printing a bisected V onto the air. A miserable little collection of lifeless-looking birds had gathered there to watch the clouds blow through the sky. Occasionally their trance was interrupted by some high-pitched squeal or another—a burst of feedback from the boom box, or a car applying its brakes—and they would lift their feet as if to shake the stiffness from their knees, trading noises like CB chatter. Sometimes that's how birds sound: electronic. Sometimes they sound like a swing set creaking against its chains. Sometimes they sound like water plinking into water. Kevin has always hated camping, hated the dirt and the smoke and the rooty ground, but once a month he sets off into the woods anyway with his Scout troop, and the birds wake him first thing in the morning, early enough that he has nothing to do but lie in his sleeping bag making comparisons while the tent gathers its soft orange light.

That one: rock salt grinding against a tire.

That one: an infant cooing for its mom.

That one: a pair of scissors *shick*ing open.

It takes forever to drive home. The evening feels less like spring than summer—dry and insecty, neverendingly sunlit. Kevin spends it in his room with his stereo, his lips shaping their way through "Hot for Teacher." Should he drop to his knees during the guitar solo? And when he says, "I brought my pencil," should he flash a yellow #2 at the crowd, like that kid with the sunglasses does in the video? Nah. Kevin owns six or seven pencils, maybe as many as a dozen, but in second grade he had scores of them, hundreds, a giant collection he accumulated by thievery. Back then he believed that as soon as an object fell to the floor, it was lost, officially. Coins, pencils, beads, barrettes—all finders-keepers. One day several kids complained that they didn't have a pencil to write with, and Jim Babb said, "That's because Kevin stole them all," and Miss Jordan made him open the pocket of his book bag, where they lay emitting their graphite smell. If only someone with a movie camera had been there to capture what her face did. For a long time it stayed poised at the edge of something, like dominoes just before they topple. Then Kevin explained that he would never have started collecting pencils in the first place if everyone else hadn't kept losing them, and her eyes, her cheeks, her jaw, her mouth—down all at once they cascaded.

It is one of those nights like a locked room, when it is impossible to imagine that time will ever pass, but time always does, and before Kevin knows it, he is circling the track that rings the football field, watching grasshoppers fling themselves out of the brush.

He has already done the fund-raising rounds, convincing his parents to make their friends, bosses, and coworkers pledge a quarter or a dollar per lap. The problem is that he doesn't care about laps—not remotely. He cares about grades and merit badges and about the thought-beams he sends out the window to Sarah Bell at night: *I love you. Pay attention to me.* He cares about Marvel and a little about DC. He cares about girls and making them laugh. That might be why he is having so much trouble monitoring his progress around the track: girls. He keeps bolting ahead to join one group, then dropping back to join another, sliding his way into the mix of a conversation for precisely as long as it takes him to pop off a joke. There are a thousand ways to be wanted, and this is his: to be amusing. Melissa Reznick says that her cat helps her stay warm at night, and Kevin tells her she's hot for creature. *Was that three laps or four? Better say four. But four isn't a round number, so five.* A few minutes later, on the highway side of the football field, with a different set of girls, he repeats the Raggedy-Ann-and-Pinocchio riddle from *Truly Tasteless Jokes*, and Margaret Casciano says, "Oh quit it you," brushing his wrist with the tips of her fingers. How can so glancing a touch feel like a bite? It's a mystery to him. He half-expects to find toothmarks on his skin. *Surely he must be up to ten by now. Ten or twelve at least.* He stops to tie his shoes, and Margaret glides away with Cathy, Kristen, Jennifer, and Tara, shrinking to half her size on the track's conveyor belt of white dirt and gravel. Kevin falls into step with Ann Harold. Ann is easy: all he has to do is power up his Coach Dale routine, and in an instant she'll be struggling not to laugh. This time she keeps herself from cracking a smile, but just barely, coming so close that her lips go all sour-lemony with the effort. Maybe at the lock-in the tornado sirens will howl, and every inch of wall space will be commandeered by other people, and the two of them will be forced to curl away together in the storage cabinet beneath the stage, wrapping themselves up in each other's arms and legs, a tight little bow-knot of body parts. *Okay. The last time he counted, he was at twelve or fifteen, and that was a few laps ago, so by now he must have reached eighteen, and eighteen might as well be twenty. Twenty-one. Let's say twenty-five.*

By the time another hour has passed, Kevin has counted seventy-five laps. Most of his friends are already hiking up the trail to school. The class schedule is broken for once, irrelevant, and since nobody is hectoring them to go inside, they stop wherever they want, on the patio or at the unpaved end of the parking lot, like anyone would anywhere. This is how a school looks when no one has anything to do: a Fourth of July party on a sun-drenched afternoon, clusters of kids layered across the landscape like figures in a View-Master reel.

A few of the guys are hanging out where the asphalt meets the dirt, some in blue jeans and some in gym shorts. Kevin edges into the circle. Right away the tailgate of a pickup begins toasting his legs. Each diamond of chrome spreads its own little thistle of light. Not until just now did it cross his mind that he should have worn his street clothes. With his shirt untucked and his shorts bagging around his thighs, he looks like he's dressed for a nap.

"What about you, Kev?" Alex asks. "How many laps did you finish?"

Kevin hopes he doesn't sound like he's bragging when he answers.

"Pffft," Shane Wesson scoffs at him. "No way. There's no fucking way on God's green fucking earth you've done eighty-one laps. Four laps equals a mile. So what you're basically saying is that you've run from here to Conway."

"I don't know what to tell you. That's how high I got."

"Man, you weren't even running all that time. I saw you. You were walking."

Kevin weasels a rock out of the dirt with his toe. He can feel the back of his neck reddening. How many laps *did* he finish? Everyone is waiting for him to answer. He ticks through his getaway options. An insult. A story. A joke. A change of subject. Nothing he can imagine would end this moment and begin another. It seems possible he will stand here prickling with self-consciousness until he dies.

"Well, how many laps did *you* do?" he asks Shane.

"Twenty-seven."

Then Bateman says, "Twenty."

And Asa. And Chuck. And Alex.

"Twenty."

"Twenty."

"Yeah, twenty."

Sometimes Kevin wishes he could take time like an egg and crack it. A year ago, the six of them went to different CACs—Bateman, Shane, and Kevin to Pleasant Valley and Asa, Alex, and Chuck to Sylvan Hills. Twenty miles of trees and pavement lay between them, full of Krogers and Burger Kings and the bending rope of the Arkansas River, green in the summer and brown in the fall, with four concrete bridges he had no earthly reason to cross. Kevin's brain has always been a kind of banker, slotting the nickel into the nickel tray and the quarter into the quarter: Bateman and Shane are old to him, Asa, Alex, and Chuck are new. Or: Bateman, Shane, and Asa have pale lips, Kevin, Alex, and Chuck have red. Or: Asa, Alex, and Chuck have sisters, Kevin and Shane have brothers. (Bateman is an only child.) Or: Shane is the tallest of them, Chuck the second tallest, Alex, Bateman, Asa, and Kevin the third, fourth, fifth, and sixth. His mind won't stop shuffling through the possibilities. But the only division that really matters is the first. Not so long ago he had never spoken to the Sylvan Hills kids, and neither had Shane or Bateman. He's thinking that there must be a version of the world where the discussion they're having now happened back then, in sixth grade, before they actually met, a version where half of them stood around talking to the ghosts of half the others, and no one knew what was going on, and it was so confusing that it didn't matter how many laps Kevin said he had run.

Suddenly 3:30 rings out over the parking lot. Though the bell is powerless this afternoon, it breaks the moment anyway. Thank God. Kevin slips out of the circle to change. The showers have been running nonstop. Their clamminess covers the locker room in a slick transparent film. The concrete floor glistens beneath the lights, gray like a bad tooth. Kevin has a hole in the knee of his blue jeans large enough to accept half his toes. The first time he tries to punch his leg through, his foot gets caught halfway down in the net of unraveling cotton. Even wearing socks, he can feel the threads flossing his toes. It's a good thing he isn't racing anyone.

"Dang it!" he complains, and someone repeats it from the other room, "Dang it!," using an angry little squeak-voice that sounds the way he sounds to himself on tape.

Some weeks go by as one long battle with anything he touches—every last cereal bowl, phone cord, and ballpoint pen. The entire world, it seems, is waiting to fall or break or tangle. Then one morning he wakes up and with no explanation he's Mary Lou Retton.

He sits down and gives his jeans another try. The coolest jeans are black or acid washed, followed by gray, followed by faded blue. Holes are cooler than no holes, buttons are cooler than zippers, Levi's are cooler than Lees, Lees are cooler than Wranglers, and Wranglers are cooler than Toughskins. It has taken him longer than average, but he is learning.

He has nothing to do after he dresses, and for a while he simply roams the halls of the building. He feels like a mouse taking a tour of its maze. Most of the school is quiet, with sparse groups of people in stairwells or open rooms producing sudden fanfares of laughter. He stops to stow his PE clothes in his locker. Behind the gym door hundreds of voices are boiling in conversation, but when he steps inside and surveys the court, he doesn't see any of his friends, just a bunch of older kids. On a whim he ducks under the bleachers, picking his way through the cat's cradle of metal reinforcements. Down here his footsteps, his coughing, his breathing, even his shirtsleeves brushing against his arms and his shoelaces tippeting over the floor, sound fuller than usual, rounder, like the echoes of other noises, great big distant booms of activity. He can hear two guys talking on the bleacher benches: "It was your fault anyway." "Fuck *you* it was my fault." "Well, it wasn't my fault, and it sure as shit wasn't Cordell's." He wonders if every building has a hiding place like this, some little pocket of space where you can listen in on people as they say whatever they say and do whatever they do. That would be totally awesome. If Kevin could vanish and reappear, if he could remain in the middle of things without anyone ever knowing, if that was his superpower and he could use it whenever he wanted, his life might be pretty good.

Hey, what if *this* was where he and Ann hid during the tornado. On second thought—no. The foxhole beneath the stage is better. Darker. A tighter fit.

Say say say what you want. Do what you do when you did what you did to me.

Eventually he ends up in the lunchroom, where Ethan and some of the others are sitting around with their butts planted flat on the tables. It's the perfect gesture of freedom, since they are defying the rules, no question, but not so badly that they'll get in trouble for it.

Kevin must have arrived in the middle of an argument about UFOs because "Here's the deal," Sean Lanham is insisting. "Let me tell you what the Bible has to say about life on other planets: nothing. Nada."

"Well," Ethan says, "no. What about Elijah's chariot?"

"What about it?"

"Some people think it was a spaceship."

"A spaceship! Dude, those were angels."

"Not necessarily."

"Angels are all over the Bible. Aliens from outer space aren't anywhere. The Old Testament: not one word. The New Testament: not one word. Don't you think God would have mentioned life on other planets if it existed?"

Kevin doesn't, and he dives in with, "God doesn't mention asteroids either. And what about dinosaurs? Automobiles, cigarettes, Indians, tacos. He doesn't mention all sorts of things. It's not like the Bible's an encyclopedia."

"Yeah, but what He does say is 'God created the heavens and the earth.' *One* earth. *This* earth."

Ethan is exasperated. "You can't possibly know that. The other planets are part of the heavens, right? Well, maybe some of them are inhabited. I'd be willing to bet on it. Maybe they have *their own* Bibles, who are you to say?"

All day long Kevin has been feeling twinges of barbed wire in his stomach whenever he thinks about the lip-synching contest, and "Hey," he asks all of a sudden, "has anyone seen Sean Hammons?" He hasn't forgotten last fall and the laryngitis incident. It would be just like Sean to get sick and go home without telling him.

No one has spoken to Sean since the bell rang. Kevin sets off to find him with a soldierly stride, his shoes announcing themselves up and down the hall, their hard slaps so forceful he thinks they should leave holes in the floor. He is prepared to march through every room of the school if he has to. But barely fifty feet away he sees Sean exiting the library, checking left and right as if for cars, with Miss Vincent stalking close behind him. And oh my God. She looks the way a mushroom looks after it rains, padded to the skin with herself, like something that was never meant to fit inside the space it was given.

"Hey! Sean!"

Sean rasps out some sort of hello to fill the pause, and with his eyes he says to Kevin, *It's not my fault.* "Um, we were just trying to find you."

Miss Vincent crosses her arms and says, "I understand the two of you have prepared a song."

"Uh-huh," Kevin answers.

"And I'm involved somehow?"

"Yeah," Kevin admits, and he fires a message back at Sean: *It was supposed to be a surprise.* Then he says it out loud: "We wanted it to be a surprise. Don't worry, you'll like it, though."

"Yes. Well. I think I'll need to make up my own mind about that."

"Oh. Yeah. You bet." Kevin leads the two of them to Mr. Garland's room. The shades drawn over the windows aerosol the air with a fine orange haze. To Kevin's eyes the desks and the trash can and the overhead projector appear to be hibernating. He could flip the switch and they would blink and stretch their limbs.

He slips the poster boards from behind one of the cabinets, standing them upright on the makeshift prop of yardsticks and cardboard he has rigged to the back. Voilà.

Miss Vincent is so quiet he can hear her breath sissing through her nostrils. Her straight skirt buckles as she cocks a hip to the side. She examines the illustration. The teeny red costume that clings to her body. The stockings with their black lines windowscreening her legs. The bunny ears rising in two pink puffs from her hair. On the poster her face is all circles and curves, dotted with black eyelashes, green eyes, and red lips, but the real one looks so flat you could paste it to the wall.

She lets out a dry little nut of a laugh. "You cannot," she says, "absolutely can*not* use that thing."

"What?" Kevin is incensed. "Why?"

"It's not remotely appropriate, for one."

"But that's not fair! Our routine doesn't make any sense without it. We practiced!"

"So sing your song. Sing it posterless."

"You can't *do* 'Hot for Teacher' without the teacher."

"Be that as it may," she says, and nabs up the drawing.

He is sure she is going to carry it off with her, but at the last second she changes her mind and hands it over to him, firmly, like the baton in a relay race. No one has ever left a room more decisively.

He listens as her footsteps fade away, then spins around. "Sean!"

"Sorry, man. Someone told her."

"What are we going to do?"

"Drop out, that's what I say. We've got like half an hour until the contest starts."

But dropping out isn't the only alternative. It can't be.

"No. Come with me. Get your boom box."

In Kevin's locker is the cassette tape containing "Hot for Teacher," a copy he recorded from the radio. He owns five or six identical blue Kmart tapes and it's possible this is the wrong one, but as soon as he fast-forwards past the final guitar licks of the song, past the crackle between tracks, and hears that staticky sound of wind and rain with those ah-ah-ahs hiccuping up from underneath, he knows immediately how he and Sean are going to win the competition. First comes the last thirty seconds of "Darling Nikki." Then comes the same thirty seconds in reverse, spun by hand from Kevin's *Purple Rain* album so that he could capture the backmasking: *Prince is fine because he knows that the Lord is coming soon.* And then comes their golden opportunity, "Let's Go Crazy," which Kevin transferred from the LP at 45 RPM, watching the needle whirlpool to the center of the turntable at double its normal speed, Prince and his helium-voice singing about elevators and the afterworld, purple bananas and Dr. Everything'll be alright.

"Okay," he says. "Here it is," and he explains the plan.

Sean gives him a pins-and-needles look. It's not his eyes—not exactly—that seem to buzz with lack of feeling, but whatever air-drawn imaginary nerves connect him to the rest of the world.

"Sean," he says, and then again, "Sean," and finally Sean sighs and says, "If you make me do this, we'll look like total idiots."

"That's a yes, though, right? It's a yes, isn't it?"

"Well . . ."

It is, and hardly a minute seems to pass before the two of them are standing in the stage lights, Sean on the guitar and Kevin at the microphone, while "Let's Go Crazy" races through its verses. The organ sounds like a tin whistle, the guitar like a chainsaw biting wood, the drums like a litter of stones rolling downhill in a barrel. Sean stands dazed at the curtain, strumming his tennis racket. Kevin bends out over the audience, chasing down faces. In the crowd he sees seniors, girls, teachers. Shane and Bateman are there, and Thad and Kenneth. He wants them so badly to want to be him. Two years ago, in fifth grade, Bateman hosted a lip-synching contest at his Halloween party, and a week before, from out of nowhere, a rumor took hold of the class that Kevin was an expert lip-syncher, destined to win with his performance of "The Longest Time." For the next few days he rehearsed like mad, perfecting every doom-bah-doo-wah and fingersnap until he almost believed it himself. No one was more disappointed than he was when he came in third. Whatever happened, he wants to know, to the hat he won at the party, with the yellow foam lightning bolts at the temples? What happened to spending the night with his friends, drinking Cokes and playing Pitfall until they passed out on the living room floor? What happened to the apartment where he and his mom lived on Sturbridge? To the house where he and his dad lived on Lakeshore? To the big brick Church of Christ building where he spent every day of his school life—in the sun when the sun was shining, in the rain when the rain was falling—with the turflike sheets of carpet in the halls, and the metal freezer filled with cartons of orange drink, and the straight line of kindergartners walking duck by duck to the water fountain? Whatever happened to two years ago?

The song ends with a last little cat-growl. Kevin leaves the stage to a smattering of applause.

Ethan lays a hand on his shoulder. "That," he says, "was truly bizarre."

And right then Kevin knows that they have lost, but when Principal McCallum counts down the winners, what he knows makes no difference, all that matters is what he wants, and he half-expects to hear his name called anyway. Third runner-up. Second. First. Only when the grand prize goes to someone else does the blood stop beating in his fingers. He shoves a hand in his pocket, fishing through the change for a Kleenex. "Well damn," he says.

Ethan sounds like a wise old man filled with his customary disappointment. "Perhaps the world simply isn't ready for Fast-Forward Prince."

And just like that, Kevin hardly cares that he lost. "Philistines."

"Give them time, give them time."

The two of them have been eating lunch together nearly every day, spending the night with each other nearly every weekend. Nothing is easier than for them to fill a few hours talking about girls and movies and comics. Colossus vs. Wolverine. Sarah vs. Annalise. Kevin buys a Sunkist and a Pay-Day from the vending machines, Ethan some Doritos and a Sprite, and they play a hunch that tonight, for once, they can roam the building eating and drinking and no one will give them a demerit. In some of the classrooms the overhead lights have been left burning. With the black sky hanging behind the windows and the floors gleaming up at the ceiling, the rows of desks and chairs seem fixed in a weird bright stillness, like trees emblazoned by lightning. Kevin zips his fingers down the fins of the lockers, creating a musical stumbling sound. The muscles in his legs, so loose at the ankles and so stiff everywhere else, make him feel like he has spent the day roller-skating. Everyone keeps calling him "eighty-one"— "Hey, eighty-one," "What's happening, eighty-one?"—and at first he has no idea why. Then all at once, in a silvery flash, he figures it out—*eighty-one laps*—and ugh. It is the wrong nickname if ever there was one. He hopes it doesn't last.

An hour or so after sunset, a teenager comes drifting through the parking lot, testing the door handles of cars. He is dressed in the blue pajamas and soft-soled slippers of a BridgeWay escapee. Kevin has never actually visited Bridge-Way, and neither has Ethan, but like everyone else, they know it is out there, a jail-like building on the far side of the woods, filled with criminals and drug addicts. Crazy people. An insane asylum.

Coach Dale hears them say so and corrects them: "Psychiatric clinic. It's a psychiatric clinic."

"Yeah. Like Arkham," Kevin says.

"Like the Holiday Inn, but for kids who need help."

As usual one of the grown-ups phones the police, but by the time the car arrives, its blue lights flickering against the side of the school, the pajama-kid has climbed the chain-link fence behind the football field and picked his way across the interstate.

It is 11:30 before everyone is corralled back onto the basketball court, and midnight before they settle into their sleeping bags. The girls are given the home side, the boys the visitors', and the teachers form a barricade along half-court. The weather is so nice that as soon as their voices die out they can hear the insects chirring through the walls, a vast sea of hopeful vibrations. Three hundred pairs of ears, Kevin thinks, and all of them listening to the same song.

He is not yet asleep, but very nearly, when everything suddenly makes perfect sense. He feels himself sailing on some great wind of thought, his mind tacking across the open water, and both of them as silver as aluminum foil, and then, in an instant, he realizes that the planet is made up of squares, blocks, cartons, boxes. He could take every piece of it—all those cereal bowls and phone cords and ballpoint pens, plus the trees and the fields, the rivers and highways, the wrenches and fire hydrants and oranges and skyscrapers, the toy trucks and weather vanes and compasses and swans, the grain silos, the mattresses, the egg crates, the elephants, the binoculars—and stack them one on top of another. They would lock together like bricks in a wall. It is so hard to describe, but important, important, he is sure of it.

The secret neatness of the world.

The plans, the blueprints.

What happened today? someone might ask him.

This, he would say.

. . . .

A wall of radiation is sweeping across Little Rock. Kevin pedals as hard as he can to outrace the fallout. His bike slices like a knife down the streets. On one side the plants are a bright May-green, their leaves twitching and swaying with every undulation of the air. On the other they hang limp and brown, as slick as tobacco slime. Slowly, ever since Chernobyl, a barricade of atomic dust has been advancing across the planet. This morning he learned from the radio that it had leapt the Mississippi into Arkansas. He wants to reach Melissa Reznick's house before the world is extinguished and the Rapture begins. He knows exactly where she lives. He lays his bike in her yard and runs to the porch, the afros of the dandelions exploding against his sneakers. "Let me in!" he shouts. "Hurry! Melissa! It's coming!" And all around him, so loud that he cannot hear his fist on the door, the sound of fire and trumpets.

He closes his eyes, then opens them. Above him he sees his bedroom's vinyl shade, carved into squares by the windowpanes and the sunlight. On his stomach the cat lies heavy as a bag of flour. It is morning, and the birds did not die in the night. Sometimes, right after he wakes up, he can feel his bed rotating brokenly beneath him, hitching back into place again and again, as if his room is tracing a thousand identical beds in the air. For a while he was somewhere else, and now he is— now he is— now he is here again, where being alive is all it takes to make him dizzy.

Usually he waits for the sensation to pass before he puts his feet to the floor, but today is the last day of school, and not only that but Ethan Carpenter is carpooling home with him to spend the night.

Ethan Carpenter. In thirteen years of best friends, he is Kevin's best yet. Easygoing and dependable. Unsecretive. Brotherly, Kevin would say, except that Kevin has a real brother, Jeff, and all they do is argue. No one other than their relatives cinches the two of them together anymore, saying their names one-two, like that, Kevin and Jeff, side by side. Every time some aunt or uncle refers to them that way, it sounds all wrong to him. These days, at school and everywhere else, it is always "Save a couple of seats for Kevin and Ethan," "Kevin and Ethan, you two fellas need to quiet down back there," "Hey, Mom, can Kevin and Ethan ride to Mazzio's with us?" They are the kind of friends who can talk for hours without tiring, contributing so quickly to each other's rolling little comic scenarios that after a while, when they build up speed, neither of them can quite remember whose jokes are whose, who shot the ball and who sank it. It seems amazing that they have known each other for so long—since first grade: Miss Emily's class—and yet they didn't *know*-know each other until this year.

Kevin steers Percy off the bed and folds back the covers. At the beginning of seventh grade, he always took a bath before bedtime. Now, nine months later, he always takes a shower before breakfast. Bit by bit, in fact, and without much effort, he has changed his whole morning routine. He parts his hair down the center now, like the older kids do, rather than at the side. He uses a facial astringent and a roll-on deodorant, so that instead of smelling like whatever he ate most recently, as he did in elementary school, he spends the day catching whiffs of fragrance from those few quick seconds of swabbing and doctoring, that chalk-and-chemical scent of Sure and Sea Breeze. Barely a month ago his penis was a small pink helmet of a thing lying against his floury skin, but last week he found himself pimpled down there with hundreds of hard white dots. At first he thought he must have a rash or an infection, a disease. Why he wasn't alarmed he couldn't say, but *Okay*, he thought, *I'm diseased now*, and decided not to tell anyone. The next day, when he discovered that the dots were growing hairs, it wasn't intelligence he felt, or even relief, just a baffled formality, as if he had woken up wearing a tie.

This morning begins like every other. He is rinsing the shampoo from his hair, though, when a flash of light pierces his eyelids and he hears the *whumpf* of a distant concussion.

Here it is: the bomb. He had convinced himself, foolishly, that it would never actually fall. Any second now and the wind will arrive, the ground will rumble, the house will shake loose from its timbers. He reaches out to wipe the water from his face and realizes that his towel has slipped off the curtain rod. All at once the thud and the brilliance make a different sort of sense. *Flash, whumpf*, of course.

His dream comes heaving back into his mind. He can visualize it in every detail. Why Melissa Reznick? he wonders.

The school day hardly seems real. Kevin sees the same group of kids as always, follows the same chain of teachers from the morning into the afternoon: Mr. Garland–Miss Vincent–Mr. Garland–Coach Dale–Mrs. Dial–Mrs. Bissard–Coach Dale. Back in August and September he kept repeating their names like that, in chronological order, for weeks, at first so that he wouldn't forget his schedule and then because the rhythm had become a kind of song in his head:

Mr. Miss. Mr. Coach. Mrs. Mrs. Coach.
Mr. Miss. Mr. Coach. Mrs. Mrs. Coach.

This is the last time he will ever have to sing it.

Between periods everyone bumps through the halls like football fans at a stadium, their voices so loud that Kevin can barely disentangle them They have no notes to jot down, no tests or quizzes to take, and neither does he, except in Bible, where Mr. Garland has given them one last memory verse. Kevin is good at quizzes, good at school. He has the instinct for learning exactly what he needs to know, then casting it aside to learn something else. He can feel himself forgetting the words of the memory verse almost as soon as they leave his pencil. Everything sinks like a rain shower into the soil.

There's always a wonderful static to his classes when he knows that he'll have a friend spending the night. Even the most boring moments of math or SRA seem to crackle around the edges. And today the feeling is twice as powerful since scarcely anything else is happening. The periods have all been shortened by ten minutes to leave time for the yearbook assembly, and at 2:30, when the bell rings, everyone pours into the gym, jamming onto the wooden bleachers. As usual the seventh graders sit all the way to the left, facing the edge of the basketball hoop, the seniors all the way to the right, facing the edge of the other basketball hoop. Kevin lets his gaze skip through the crowd. William Carpenter with his back as straight as a yardstick. Leigh Cushman with those curls of hair at his neck. Sarah Bell with her fruit-red lips. Once upon a time, when they were kids, her picture was directly next to his in the yearbook. Their names made sure of it—Sarah Bell and then Kevin Brockmeier. He liked to pretend they were boyfriend and girlfriend, holding hands beneath their photos. He imagined her thumb stroking his palm, her pretty knee meeting his handsome one. The two of them were in love, madly and deeply and lastingly in love, down there where no one could see them. Buzzing with their eagerness to touch. To burrow in and add their temperatures together.

Kiss her picture and she'd feel your lips on her cheek.

Close the pages and you'd turn out the lights.

The game didn't end until fifth grade, when a new kid, Michael Berridge, joined the class's alphabet. These days there must be a half dozen faces wedged between them: at one end there is Sarah, and then, like drawings of the presidents on a ruler, there are Sharon Benton and Jim Boothby and Alex Braswell and God knows who else, and finally, a row or more away, there is Kevin. It's hopeless.

Everyone waits for the teachers to finish unboxing the yearbooks. They work from receipts taped to the covers, haphazardly calling out names. When they reach Kevin's, he cuts across the sideline to the card table. The books are bound in purple and gold, the school colors, and decorated with overlapping horseshoes—mustang shoes—the school mascot. He flips to his photo, and thank God he's smiling.

For the rest of the hour, he roams the building targeting signatures:

How's it going Kev!? It's been nice knowing you this year ↟ you've been a good friend. You are very smart. <u>Ethan</u>
1st to sign   ↵

Kevin, You are the sweetest boy in this school. Love ya, Ann

Glad we were good friends. Wish you didn't have that trouble at the first of the year. Hope you don't next year. Keep up the <u>good</u> grades. Chuck
P.S. You're an awesome poet.

You are a polse, Kevin! Leigh C.
I mean that.

Hey Kevin I know I'll see you this summer, but then again you might be at your dad's so stay cool and see you next year. Your friend, Michael Berridge

Kevin, a smart and funny guy you are. If get stupid and dress out slower you would be me. Dan

Kevin, I don't know you all that well, but I do know you are very sweet and SMART! Love ya, Meredith

Kevin, Stay stupid. J/J. Looking forward to next year. Love ya, Lisa

Kevin, You have been too nice to me! I don't know where to begin! You're also the kindest person. I can never repay you. If I can't go here, keep in touch. Love ya, Carina

All the girls end their notes the same way: "Love ya." But they don't love him—not really. The giveaway is the missing *I.* "*I* love ya" would mean that they actually loved him. "Love ya" just means that they're out there loving.

He thinks it is funny to sign his own yearbook, so he scrawls, "You're cool!" and prints his name underneath. Then he makes his way upstairs to Miss Vincent's room. She is angled over a stack of papers, writing B+, B+, A–, holding her ballpoint pen lightly between two fingers, so that the blunt end twitches and sways as she works, carving exuberant shapes in the air. He wonders if it's drawing the same grades at the top that it is at the bottom.

"Miss Vincent?" he says.

She pronounces his name, "Kevin Brockmeier," with the hushed tone of an announcer at a tennis match.

"Will you sign my yearbook?"

"Can there be any doubt?"

Half the time he has no idea whether he understands what she's saying. Little breezes seem to blow through her voice, jogging it this way and that like something with wings, and no matter how nimbly he reaches, he can never quite grasp it. But he has learned a trick with questions, one that works almost every time, which is that you can shuffle their words around to concoct a safe answer. *Can there be any doubt?* "There can be no doubt," he says.

Miss Vincent grimaces and makes a not-so-sure gesture. "Well, maybe there can be *some* doubt."

"Yeah, maybe . . ."

"Here," she tells him. "I'm teasing. Give me your yearbook." After she returns it, she adds, "You take care of yourself this summer. And next year, too, okay? I've gotten to know you. You treat people sympathetically. You deserve good things."

"You're welcome. You too."

Man! He has never been able to converse with grown-ups

the way he does with ordinary people. Sooner or later, he is always convinced, he will break some hidden rule and they will laugh or give a wordless frown—or, worse, embarrass him with a correction. *No, Kevin. Nuh-uh. It's like this.* He can hardly utter a sentence without bracing himself for his next mistake. His shoulders hunch and his stomach tightens—not much, but noticeably. It is impossible for him to relax. There are days when it takes all his willpower just to keep his eyes from stinging. He lives in a giant world of men and women. Sometimes there's no ignoring it. What if he disappoints them somehow? What if they decide they don't like him anymore? It would be no more mysterious than the fact that they ever did.

He leaves down the empty back stairs. At the bottom he nudges the door open with his hip. The sound of conversation microphones open around him. Something must be wrong with the air-conditioning, because the lunchroom is freezing cold. Clusters of kids prop themselves against the tables and the vending machines, their bodies doing an aching little up-down motion. An older girl—Chuck's sister—cups her palms to her mouth and breathes into them at 98.6 degrees. One of the football players, a stocky guy whose name Kevin doesn't know, stands with his hands tucked into his sleeves like an Indian squaw. Along the side wall, leaning against the windows, are Thad and Kenneth, Craig Bell and Clint Fulkerson, Shane Wesson, Shane Roper, Joseph Rimmer, Levon Dollard, the whole bunch of them too absorbed in whatever joke they are telling to have noticed Kevin standing just a few feet away. In his Goon voice, with that strange kazoo-hum, Thad says, "Will you sign my queerbook?" and then in his regular voice, "No! No! Rearbook! Will you sign my *rear-book*?" and it must be the ideal line, because everyone booms with laughter.

Thad is (1) slick, (2) happy, and (3) confident. He is (4) handsome, in an Adam's-appley sort of way. And he is (5) mean, or at least (5) inaccessible, or how about (1, 2, 3, 4, 5) Kevin doesn't know him at all anymore.

At the beginning of seventh grade, they were best friends, but the months kept changing, no one could stop them. Their friendship blew up and—*flash, whumpf*—filled the atmosphere. The dust of it has been chasing him ever since.

He was hoping he could avoid seeing Thad and Kenneth and the others before the final bell rang. He considers backing out and returning upstairs, following the convolutions of the building to the foyer. It is amazing how long a second can last. But the sun is laying a stripe of yellow light across the room, one that climbs the benches and scales the tables, then plunges to the floor like the skyline of a city. He walks right through it, and no one seems to notice.

> Kevin — I guess it is needless for me to say that you are an excellent student. It has been so much fun having you in class and being able to share in your creative efforts. I have also been pleased that you are coming out more and are more outgoing. You are such a fun student and a pleasure to know. Keep trying and succeeding. Love, Miss Vincent

Half an hour later he and Ethan are home on Northwick Court, drinking Capri Suns from the refrigerator as they recline on the back porch. The end of school must have worked its spell, because everything feels different. Quieter.

More yielding. Some switch has flipped inside the day: a few hours ago it was warm and shining like spring, and now it is warm and shining like summer. They listen to the fan whir inside the air conditioner, then spin to a stop as the thermostat clicks off. They watch Percy track a pair of dragonflies across the lawn, leaping at them with his paws outstretched. Thousands of glowing white specks dance over the grass, and tangles of honeysuckle rustle against the fence, and the shadows of the clouds are like the shadows water makes as it ripples over gravel.

As soon as they finish their drinks, Kevin coaxes Ethan into playing a kick-game in the carport. Ricochet, he calls it, and all it takes is a soccer ball and a good hard wall. The ball rebounds off the bricks with a weirdly tinny smack, the sound of an echo with nowhere to go. It launches itself at their legs, careering into the door and the mailbox, the pillar and the bushes. Every few kicks it clips past them and sails out of bounds down the driveway.

After they become tired of chasing it, they decide to hike to Osco and spend their money, following a shortcut Kevin knows through the woods. He has been walking to the same drugstore since he was in kindergarten—no matter which house or apartment he has lived in, and no matter with which of his parents—buying comic books and stickers, Choose Your Own Adventure novels, cinnamon oil for toothpicks. A bag boy is collecting shopping carts from the metal corrals and wheeling them across the parking lot, a long square millipede of a creature that keeps hitching and shuddering over the asphalt. Kevin and Ethan are busy kicking rocks, and even though they veer back and forth to chase after the strays, wincing at the ones that ping against the undersides of cars, it doesn't matter—they still beat the bag boy to the sidewalk by a mile. The candy aisle is midway through the store: rack after rack of chocolate bars and chewing gum. Ethan chooses a box of Nerds, Kevin one of Everlasting Gobstoppers—fifty-nine cents plus tax, and that's it for his allowance—and then they riffle through the books and the magazines. *Mad* and *Cracked. Hit Parader* and *Song Hits.* Stephen R. Donaldson. Stephen King. *Snappy Answers to Stupid Questions.*

The two of them have already set out for home when Ethan says, "You do know you have a zit on your face."

"No, there isn't. Where?" Kevin finds it near the tip of his nose: a hard round pill of skin. "Jesus! It's like a candy button."

Ethan tries to tie off his smile. "I think it adds character."

"Shut up. Go to hell."

Kevin doesn't need his fingers to feel the tightness of the thing, the weight, but he can't quite catch sight of it. Attempting to do so only makes him aware of the way his nose hovers between his eyes, bulging there like an orange wedge. How does anyone ever manage to see anything else?

"At least your yearbook picture came out all right," Ethan says. "Look at what they did to me."

It's true: a printing flaw on the page has marked Ethan's cheek with a horrible black ink flag.

"I think it adds character," Kevin says.

"Shut up."

Soon it is dinnertime, and then snack time and TV time, and then Kevin's brother has gone to bed, and then his mom, and he and Ethan use the rails of the wooden fence to climb onto the roof of the house. Once, not so long ago, there were no buildings at this end of town, no houses, only acres of empty fields and a loose net of oak trees, and every time Kevin hoists himself onto the shingles, his mind offers up the same idea: how if he had been here back then—*right* here, exactly where he is now—he would have been pacing through a canopy of branches, arranging his body in midair. Maybe that's where ghost stories come from, he thinks. Maybe ghosts are just people walking around in the past. People at the wrong time.

He and Ethan lie back on the slanting tiles and stretch out over the kitchen. Beneath them must be the cabinet where his mom keeps the oils and the spices, and beneath that the counter with the tall wooden stools, and beneath that the tortoise-green arabesque of the linoleum. They prop their heads on their arms, switching every so often from the right to the left, using their shirts to brush the roof-grit off their skin. A car guns its engine on Reservoir, and a stereo plays across the street at the Stegalls', but otherwise the night has a beautiful grassy stillness to it. All they can hear is the chiming of the insects, a sound so full and layered it's easy to imagine it cascading down from outer space. The moon is hole punching the sky, the stars salting it in little collections of four and five. Even the very closest ones, Kevin has read, are light-years upon light-years away. How many of them have shed their surfaces already, he wonders, and how many have collapsed? How many stars must go out before a constellation dies?

"What's the best nightmare you've ever had?" he asks Ethan.

"The best?"

"The worst."

"Hmm. I'll have to get back to you on that."

Kevin tells him about the Chernobyl dream—the fallout and the blaze of light, his three-speed and Melissa Reznick. He shakes a Gobstopper from the box. "Okay, let's say this: there's a nuclear war, and you've got an island in the middle of the ocean. You can save five people. Who do you take with you?"

"Five people including me?"

"Five people *in addition* to you," Kevin clarifies, and names his own five: Ethan, Sarah, Melissa, Bateman, "and Carina," he finishes. "No—Ann. No!—Carina."

"So no one in your family?"

"Oh!"

"No room for your family on the island. Tough luck, family! You can go ahead and burn to cinders."

Well, no, but his family would overturn the whole question. "Let's say our families are already taken care of."

"All right. Then you and Bateman, and I guess Chuck, and Jennifer, and Shane Wesson."

"Shane *Wesson*?"

Ethan is the kind of person whose entire personality flashes through in his laugh, quiet, calm, and unpretentious, as if somewhere deep inside his body he is always cushioned in an old recliner with a comic book propped open on his chest.

"Be serious."

"Okay, okay. Clay Carpenter."

"Good answer. So are you saying you *like* Jennifer?"

"I don't like anybody right now."

"Huh. I don't think there's ever been a single time in my life when I didn't like anybody."

Ethan laughs again. "Yeah, I know that about you. So when did you say you leave for your dad's?"

"Shit. Wednesday. Man, I don't want to go to Mississippi. Everything always changes when I'm in Mississippi."

"Well, we've still got a few days left. I have all this stuff to do tomorrow, and Sunday is Sunday, but what are your plans Monday?"

"Yeah! Do you think your mom would drop you off? That would be excellent. I get paid tomorrow. We could go see a movie."

"I'll ask her."

Last summer Kevin was leaving for Mississippi, and *Gotcha!* had just opened, and "Everybody Wants to Rule the World" was the number-one song on the radio. Now he is leaving for Mississippi, and *Top Gun* has just opened, and "West End Girls" is the number-one song on the radio.

The Gobstopper clacks against his teeth, and he takes it out to inspect the colors. Though the streetlamps have dimmed on their timers, the light is still bright enough for him to see the miniature swirling planet the layers have formed, some Jupiter floating far up in the night. He tucks the candy back in his cheek, then crosses his hands behind his head.

"Thad called it a queerbook," he says.

"Did what?"

"It doesn't matter."

Someone's tires whisper past on the road, and suddenly Kevin's mind carries him back to Monday morning, when the sixth-graders paid their year-end visit to the school's main campus. How nervous they must have been as their bus coasted to a stop in the parking lot, yet how carefully, he thinks, they hid it, slouching in their seats and trading jokes with their friends. On one side of the river stood the brown-brick building where they had grown up playing war and inventing fan clubs at recess, on the other the redbrick building where half the students drove their own cars. Between them lay five minutes of curving highway and sandstone bluffs and hillsides green with a million trees. The kids descended the bus platform onto the patio and jostled through the school's front doors. The halls absorbed their footsteps. The crowd rolled around them like a wave. And in chapel, when Principal McCallum said, "Now will you all please join me in the Mustang Anthem," they sang so much louder than everyone else—

> We clasp our hands in unity.
> Our hearts are joined in love.
> We make our pledge of loyalty
> To Him who dwells above.
> And as we meet life's fortunes here,
> Our thoughts shall always be
> Of love for each and every year
> We share at CAC.

Kevin listened to their voices reflecting off the rafters, a great unanimous chorus of pre-altos and pre-tenors. Even the coolest of them had not yet learned that it was better not to demand too much attention. A year ago he was one of them and had no idea where his life was going. As the next song began, he sat in the bleachers remembering what it was like. Thinking, Before you know it, nothing will be the same. Saying, You're not me yet, but I'm still you.

Acknowledgments

I owe thanks to the William F. Laman Public Library for a fellowship that allowed me to complete this book, as well as to my editor, Edward Kastenmeier, and his colleagues Tim O'Connell, Jocelyn Miller, and Emily Giglierano; to my agent, Jennifer Carlson, and her associates at Dunow, Carlson & Lerner; to my publicist, Josie Kals; my production editor, Victoria Pearson; and everyone else at Pantheon and Vintage; to the editors of the various magazines in which portions of this book were originally published, most especially Carol Ann Fitzgerald and Marc Smirnoff at *The Oxford American*, Meghan McCarron at *Interfictions,* Stephen Corey and Jenny Gropp Hess at *The Georgia Review*, Rachael Allen and Yuka Iqarashi at *Granta,* and Aja Gabel and Karyna McGlynn at *Gulf Coast*; to Jessica Easto and Chris Bertram for helping me in my hunt for a title; to Jessica Brogdon for refreshing my memory; and to Karen Russell for responding to this odd little memoir-thing with enthusiasm, sympathy, and acuity.

In addition to *A Few Seconds of Radiant Filmstrip,* Kevin Brockmeier is the author of the novels *The Illumination, The Brief History of the Dead,* and *The Truth About Celia;* the story collections *Things That Fall from the Sky* and *The View from the Seventh Layer;* and the children's novels *City of Names* and *Grooves: A Kind of Mystery.* His work has been translated into seventeen languages. He has published his stories in such venues as *The New Yorker, The Georgia Review, McSweeney's, Zoetrope, Tin House, The Oxford American, The Best American Short Stories, The Year's Best Fantasy and Horror,* and *New Stories from the South.* He has recieved the Borders Original Voices Award, three O. Henry Awards (one, a first prize), the PEN USA Award, a Guggenheim Fellowship, and an NEA Grant. In 2007, he was named one of *Granta* magazine's Best Young American Novelists He teaches frequently at the Iowa Writers' Workshop, and he lives in Little Rock, Arkansas, where he was raised.

A NOTE ON THE TYPE

This book was set in Old Style No. 7. This face is based on types designed and cut by the celebrated Edinburgh typefounders Miller & Richard in 1860. Old Style No. 7, composed in a page, gives a subdued color and an even texture that make it easily and comfortably readable.

Composed by North Market Street Graphics,
Lancaster, Pennsylvania

Printed and bound by Berryville Graphics,
Berryville, Virginia

Designed by M. Kristen Bearse